CYCLING
CLIMBS
OF THE
MIDLANDS

A ROAD CYCLIST'S GUIDE

SIMON WARREN

F

FRANCES
LINCOLN

Frances Lincoln Limited
A subsidiary of Quarto Publishing Group UK
74–77 White Lion Street
London
N1 9PF

A catalogue record for this book is available from the British Library.

978-0-7112-3706-3

Printed and bound in China

1 2 3 4 5 6 7 8 9

Quarto is the authority on a wide range of topics.

Quarto educates, entertains and enriches the lives of
our readers – enthusiasts and lovers of hands-on living.

www.QuartoKnows.com

Thanks to my family and friends for their continued support
and patience while I persist in trying to ride every hill in Britain.
Thanks to all those on social media who have suggested climbs
for me to seek out – you led me to some real gems. And finally
thanks to anyone else who helped bring this book to life.

CONTENTS

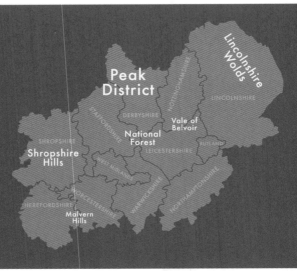

Peak
District

Lincolnshire
Wolds

NOTTINGHAMSHIRE

LINCOLNSHIRE

STAFFORDSHIRE

DERBYSHIRE

Vale of
Belvoir

National
Forest

RUTLAND

SHROPSHIRE

WEST MIDLANDS

LEICESTERSHIRE

Shropshire
Hills

WORCESTERSHIRE

WARWICKSHIRE

NORTHAMPTONSHIRE

HEREFORDSHIRE

Malvern
Hills

THE MIDLANDS

Born in Cosford, to the west of Wolverhampton, and raised just outside Newark in Nottinghamshire, the Midlands are my homeland. My formative years as a cyclist were spent either lost on the plains of Lincolnshire or being battered by winds in the Vale of Belvoir. Each road within a 50-kilometre radius of Newark holds a memory of a battle won or lost, of wheat fields in the summer sun, or punctures mended in the driving rain. As you work through the hills in the first chapter you will notice that the text is littered with autobiographical references. Apologies if they seem quite frequent, but you'll

know as well as I do that you form a special bond with your local roads. The lanes that test you day in day out can become your best friends, and your worst enemies.

The first chapter kicks off in the Wolds of Lincolnshire: a tiny, raised ridge conveniently placed to provide the locals with some much needed elevation. Those of you lucky enough to live in the Lake District or the Yorkshire Dales may scoff at the pitiful lumps that pass for hills in these parts. If you live east of Lincoln, though, these climbs are your mountains, and there are just enough of them to string together a pretty tough ride.

I didn't venture to the Wolds that often in my youth; most of my time was spent riding closer to home, in the Vale of Belvoir. And in particular climbing the toughest hill there: the one and only Terrace Hill. This climb was where it all began; it was the catalyst for my love of climbing, and the first place I won a bike race, so it will always have a very special place in my heart.

Chapter Two is devoted entirely to the most voluptuous county in the region, Derbyshire. Filled with legendary roads such as Mam Nick, Monsal Head, and the sensational Winnats Pass, there isn't an inch of flat to be found anywhere. Back in the 1980s my weekends away would take my friends and I from Newark to the youth hostel in Castleton on a pilgrimage to ride Winnats. I'll never forget my first ascent one cold

November morning. With a sore head from the youthful excess of the night before, we rolled out of Castleton to face one of the most daunting roads in the country. On the old winter clunker with a 42x23 bottom gear, would I make it? Of course I would – I was 18 years old, under 10 stone, and couldn't get enough of it!

In the summer months we would plan regular raids into Derbyshire, heading to Matlock or Bakewell to fill our legs with climbs before returning, aching, to the flat plains of home. Then in October we'd go back to race up them, which is where my passion for Riber began (see page 58). It's an affair that may have lost some of its lustre over the years now I'm no longer able to cover the race distance in less than four minutes, but it will always be one of my favourite roads.

Moving on from Derbyshire I headed into an area of the country I'd rarely visited by bike, the West Midlands. There are many areas of high ground spread round the region, most obviously tracing the border with Wales from Oswestry down into Hereford. Filled with sharp ups and downs it was tough to make the final selection and I was forced to omit a few beauties in the final cut. Once I'd searched round the border I next set my gaze on the Shropshire Hills where one particular climb caught my eye: the service road up to the radio masts on top of Brown Clee Hill. I checked online to make sure it could be ridden. I knew it was going to be a tough climb, but I'd failed to study the gradient in detail – what a big mistake. Averaging 18% for 600m it's the single toughest stretch of straight climbing I have yet to find. Harder than Hardknott

and more brutal than Bealach-Na-Bà – not because it's steeper, but because there are no bends! I'm afraid to say I had to stop and walk three times; the 39x26 gear that I had at my disposal simply wasn't small enough, and my legs didn't want any of it. No climb beats me and gets away with it, though, so a couple of weeks later I returned with the best bike to get my revenge. This time I made it to the top without unclicking, but I can't deny that the thought crossed my mind. It is total and utter torment.

Before you start I'd like to apologise for the lack of sunshine in the photos. It rained so much while I rode these roads that I almost grew flippers and gills. I hope you have better weather, but even if you don't you'll still find seventy-five killer roads to test your legs. So get out there and 'Ride them all'.

1:14.2

Many have tried, but all have failed. The imperious time of one minute, fourteen point two seconds has stood solid, resolute in the face of all challengers since 1981. Malcolm Elliott's record for the Monsal Hill Climb is one of the longest standing in British cycling, and at the time of publication the closest anyone has got come to beating it was in 2003 when Russell Downing posted one minute, eighteen point three seconds. First run in 1930, past winners include Tom Simpson, Darryl Webster, Granville Sydney, and both Dean and Russell Downing. It's a title all riders would love to have on their palmarès, but only a few have the magic ingredients to nail it.

The current custodians of the event, the Sheffrec CC, under the leadership of Marc Etches, have turned what was already a popular race into a must-ride (and must-spectate) day on the cycling calendar. The maximum gradient is a substantial but not leg-breaking 17%, and at only 500m long it favours both the lightweights and the explosive sprinters. Riders who would never be classed as climbers but who have bags of raw power can destroy this course, making a mockery of gravity and taking the scalps of the mountain goats along the way.

If you choose to race you can split the hill into three distinct sectors. First is 'the flat bit'. You launch yourself from the starting hold like a ball from a cannon and spin effortlessly, full of adrenaline, towards the base of the rise. The instant the road tips up, nature's forces begin to pull you back and you begin the second part, 'the silence'. There may be a sprinkling of spectators down here but most likely it will be just you, your laboured breathing, and your ever-quickening heartbeat. This is the toughest part of the climb and it requires immense willpower to absorb the pain and continue riding at 100%.

As the road begins to bend right, and the grassy bank on your left fills with crowds, you are now in the third and final sector, 'the canyon of noise'. From here on there's no pain; no matter how much the lungs burn and the legs scream, the cacophony of vocal support from behind the barriers cancels it out. You can now dig deeper than you ever could in training, because each single voice is like a hook that wraps itself round your handlebars and drags you upwards. If you've ever wondered how the pros climb the mountains so fast, then here is your answer. Push that gear over those last few yards, make the abrupt kink left to cross the line, and then (with every sinew in your body about to explode) pick your way through the bustle at the top in search of air and the relief of flat land. If you love suffering and the taste of blood, and enjoy seeing your fellow man contorted with pain, then get yourself to the Monsal Hill Climb – you will not be disappointed.

!

REMEMBER
to check
your bike, check
your body, wear
a helmet, and, above
all, have fun!

20%

**DANGEROUS
HILL**

Weight limit
7·5 Tonnes
2$\frac{1}{2}$ miles ahead
No thro' route to A6
for H·G·V·S·

LEGEND

LOCATIONS

You will be able to locate each hill from the small maps provided: simply, **S** marks the start and **F** marks the finish. I would suggest you invest in either Ordnance Survey maps or a GPS system to help plan your routes in more detail. The grid reference in the Factfile locates the summit of each climb, and in brackets is the relevant **OS Landranger** map. The graphic at the start of each chapter will show you where the hills lie in the context of each region.

TIMINGS

Each Factfile includes the approximate time needed to ride each hill. Timed over the distance marked, this is how long it took me to complete each climb at a reasonable but comfortable pace. Since I rode in all weathers, from blizzards to baking heat, I have adjusted the times slightly to accommodate for the adverse conditions I faced on the day. The times could be used as a target but are really just intended to help you plan your rides.

FACTFILE

WHERE From the centre of Bakewell head east on Bridge Street, over the River Wye then take the first right on to Station Road to begin the climb.

GRID REF SK 229 695 (**OS**119)

LENGTH 2150m

HEIGHT GAIN 155m

APPROX CLIMB TIME 8.5mins

RATINGS

The climbs are rated from **1/10** to **10/10** within the context of the book. The rating is an amalgamation of gradient, length, the likely hostility of the riding conditions, and the condition of the surface. All the climbs are tough, therefore **1/10** equals 'hard', and **10/10** equals 'it's all you can do to keep your bike moving'. Some will suit you more than others; the saying 'horses for courses' applies, but all the **10/10** climbs will test any rider.

MAP KEY

Motorway	M1
A Road	A123
B Road	B1234
Minor Road	
Rail line	STATION
Hill route	START
	S — F FINISH
Town	TOWN
Scale	2km

11

EAST
MIDLANDS

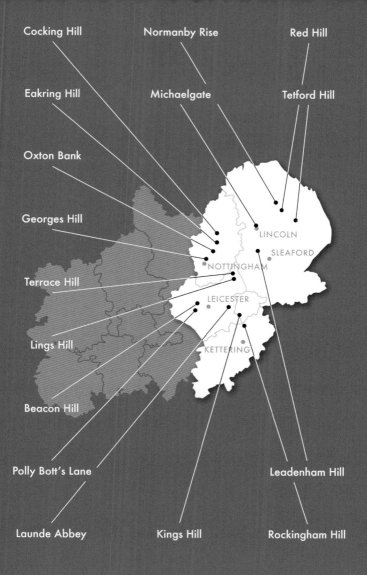

Cocking Hill

Normanby Rise

Red Hill

Eakring Hill

Michaelgate

Tetford Hill

Oxton Bank

Georges Hill

LINCOLN

SLEAFORD

Terrace Hill

NOTTINGHAM

LEICESTER

Lings Hill

KETTERING

Beacon Hill

Polly Bott's Lane

Leadenham Hill

Launde Abbey

Kings Hill

Rockingham Hill

NORMANBY RISE

NORMANBY LE WOLD, LINCOLNSHIRE

To the east of Market Rasen lie the Lincolnshire Wolds, a veritable mountain range rising from agricultural plains. A climber's paradise protruding from the humdrum of the flatlands. Have I sold it enough yet? OK, of course they aren't mountains, but if you search you will find some slopes to test the legs and there are few better than this climb: Normanby Rise. Leaving the A46, you cross the rail line and ride into Claxby; as the road bends left on to Mulberry Road you leave it to head straight on. As you rise, the gradient increases until you find yourself clicking rapidly through the sprockets. Gently weaving first left and then right, there is a brow ahead in front of a lone house. This isn't the top, but it offers you a brief rest before you begin the final stretch. Bending 90 degrees left and then straight away right, you hit the best part of the climb between tall hedgerows ahead of the summit at the junction.

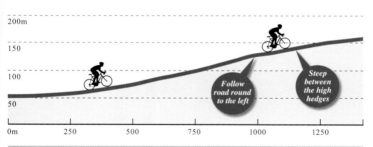

Follow road round to the left

Steep between the high hedges

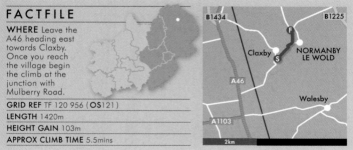

FACTFILE

WHERE Leave the A46 heading east towards Claxby. Once you reach the village begin the climb at the junction with Mulberry Road.

GRID REF TF 120 956 (**OS**121)

LENGTH 1420m

HEIGHT GAIN 103m

APPROX CLIMB TIME 5.5mins

RED HILL

STENIGOT, LINCOLNSHIRE

What would constitute an insignificant lump in a more voluptuous part of Britain makes for a serious climb around here. But don't simply dismiss it – this road has plenty of character, with a more than sufficient gradient to make those legs burn. Leaving the T-junction at the bottom you immediately pass a 10% gradient sign, and there aren't many of those in Lincolnshire, so be warned. The gentle approach to the steep stuff is arrow-straight and then where it kinks right it starts to rise more rapidly. The surface is lovely and smooth, climbing in the shadow of the tall, grassy bank on your left that's capped with a chalky outcrop. Continuing to bend right, the road then heads left where it reaches its 10% maximum up to a small parking space on the left. The climbing isn't over yet but it's very mild, so stick it in the big ring and push on hard to the true summit at the junction with Hall Lane.

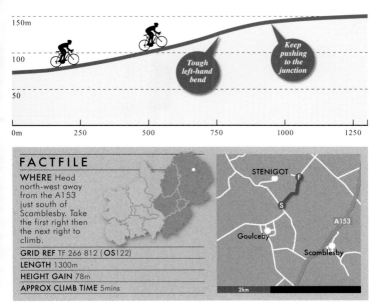

FACTFILE

WHERE Head north-west away from the A153 just south of Scamblesby. Take the first right then the next right to climb.

GRID REF TF 266 812 (OS122)

LENGTH 1300m

HEIGHT GAIN 78m

APPROX CLIMB TIME 5mins

TETFORD HILL

TETFORD, LINCOLNSHIRE

Lying on the southern flank of the Wolds and rising from a sleepy village in a very sleepy part of England is a vertical trap just waiting to snare its next victim. I wouldn't say this is the toughest climb in Lincolnshire, but it's certainly up there. You climb a little as you leave the village and then level out as the road bends 90 degrees left and then right to face the ridge ahead – the gateway to the Wolds. Carry on along the flat plain until you reach the first house, where the climb kicks off. It's not instantly steep, but before long it approaches 14%. There is a slight easing after this first kick and from then on it's a solid test of the legs and lungs. There are no significant bends, just a gentle curve round to the left up past the entrance to an abandoned quarry. Following the high, grassy banks on your right you'll soon see the welcome brow; force your way up and over and then pinch yourself. Are you really in Lincolnshire?

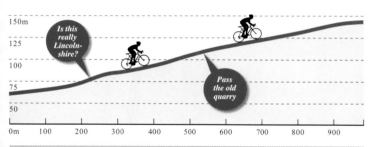

FACTFILE

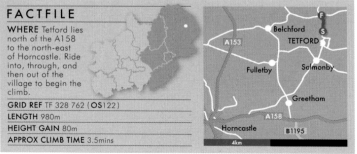

WHERE Tetford lies north of the A158 to the north-east of Horncastle. Ride into, through, and then out of the village to begin the climb.

GRID REF TF 328 762 (OS122)

LENGTH 980m

HEIGHT GAIN 80m

APPROX CLIMB TIME 3.5mins

MICHAELGATE

Michaelgate is a true classic – a 1-in-6 cobbled road through the heart of Lincoln. The centrepiece of the annual Lincoln Grand Prix, one of the country's greatest bike races, this is a bone-shaking, lung-busting test of both man and machine. Finding the base of the climb in the maze of little streets is a challenge in itself; there are a number of cobbled hills here including the even steeper but, unfortunately, pedestrianised Steep Hill. The cobbles are well maintained and even but can be slippery; the key is to keep your momentum and stay seated to increase traction. There is a foot of smooth paving between the stones and the curb, just enough to ride on, but this takes the fun out of the climb so stick to the stones. Once up the main section you plateau. The way is pedestrianised up ahead so bear left onto Wordsworth Street and follow it up to the junction with Drury Lane. Turn right here to follow the race route into Castle Square.

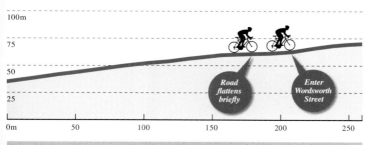

Road flattens briefly

Enter Wordsworth Street

100m

75

50

25

0m   50   100   150   200   250

FACTFILE

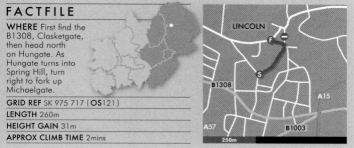

WHERE First find the B1308, Clasketgate, then head north on Hungate. As Hungate turns into Spring Hill, turn right to fork up Michaelgate.

GRID REF SK 975 717 (**OS**121)

LENGTH 260m

HEIGHT GAIN 31m

APPROX CLIMB TIME 2mins

LINCOLN

B1308

A57

A15

B1003

250m

LEADENHAM HILL

Growing up in Nottinghamshire, this climb was one of the key landmarks on family trips to the coast. Back then it was still the main road, but now a bypass navigates the A17 round the village of Leadenham. And, as I'm mentioning the A17, I must warn you that this is a truly horrible road to cycle on – it is constantly full of HGVs hauling produce from Lincolnshire's farms, so keep your time on it to a minimum. The approach to the hill starts pan flat and then you begin the first half of the climb, rising sharply to finish in front of the George Hotel. Turn right here and then left towards the traffic lights at the junction with the A607. If you're lucky you'll pass right through – if not, just enjoy the rest. The second half of the climb is tougher as it arcs right and then left, up through the wood. Give it some stick as you exit the trees and keep pushing over the pronounced brow to reach the transmitter just off to the left.

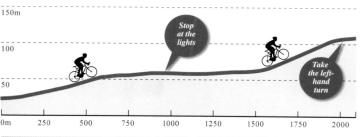

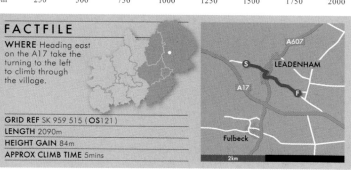

FACTFILE

WHERE Heading east on the A17 take the turning to the left to climb through the village.

GRID REF SK 959 515 (OS121)
LENGTH 2090m
HEIGHT GAIN 84m
APPROX CLIMB TIME 5mins

COCKING HILL

KIRTON, NOTTINGHAMSHIRE

I rode this once during the early stages of a big local bike race. I managed to blag a ride because my club was the promoter, but the event was way out of my league. This was made painfully evident as the pros pottered up chatting while those at the back were breathing out of their ears. The hill is no giant, but it's perfect for hill intervals and just steep enough to make you hurt good and proper. Leaving Ollerton you reach an abrupt left-hand bend where you must leave the main road and head straight on. Take care at the junction and then head up under the rail bridge. Passing the entrance to the brickworks, the slope begins to pick up, but it's not steep until you reach the second road on the left. From here it's tough into the small woodland where up ahead twin signs stand either side of the road like a gateway to the summit. Climb past these to meet the first of two brows and then press on to the finish on the agricultural plateau.

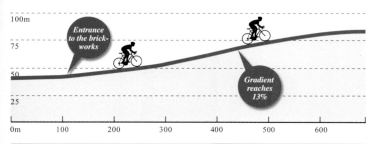

FACTFILE

WHERE Head east out of Ollerton on the A6075 through Boughton. As you approach a 90-degree bend, turn right and climb up under the bridge.

GRID REF SK 693 674 (OS120)

LENGTH 690m

HEIGHT GAIN 48m

APPROX CLIMB TIME 2.5mins

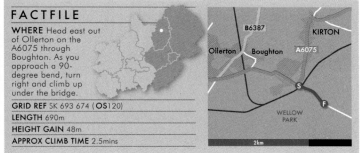

RATING 1/10

EAKRING HILL

It's reasonably lumpy in this part of Notts and Eakring is my favourite hill to ride. In 2004, after ten years away from racing, I ended up at its base to start my 'comeback'. Our club had historically used Terrace Hill (see page 33) for its annual championships, but in my absence they'd gone soft and relocated here. Eakring Hill does require a fair effort to climb, but sadly it's not as tough as Terrace, and I have voiced my opinion clearly. To tackle it, leave the A617 west of Kirklington then step on the gas as you cross the small stream. The incline is mild and then bites slightly before almost levelling beside a lone house. Here's where the challenge begins. Bending left and then sweeping right, the gradient builds to hit its maximum of 10% between the high hedges. Snaking left and right, keep the pressure on and focus ahead at the point where the road bends left, as that's the summit.

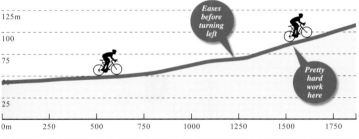

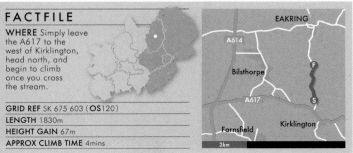

FACTFILE

WHERE Simply leave the A617 to the west of Kirklington, head north, and begin to climb once you cross the stream.

GRID REF SK 675 603 (OS120)

LENGTH 1830m

HEIGHT GAIN 67m

APPROX CLIMB TIME 4mins

OXTON BANK

OXTON, NOTTINGHAMSHIRE

The first bike race I ever witnessed – Newark Castle's Chairman's Chase – came up this hill. The whole family turned out because my uncle, the club's finest time trialist, was riding, and naturally we had high hopes for him. Unfortunately his stocky frame was no match for the whippet climbers and we were disappointed to see him propping up the rear of the peloton as it surged past. Personally I must have ridden the climb a hundred times in training; it was the closest decent hill to my parents' home, so I know it inside out and back to front. You leave Oxton and ahead the road kinks right up the hillside into the trees. Hold back slightly as it begins to rise. It eases a touch when you hit the snaking bends and then ramps up – here is where you give it some gas. It's a minute flat out, on the rivet, until you reach the brow, where it's one last push before the fantastic 6-kilometre descent into Southwell.

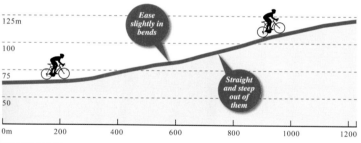

Ease slightly in bends

Straight and steep out of them

125m
100
75
50
0m

0m   200   400   600   800   1000   1200

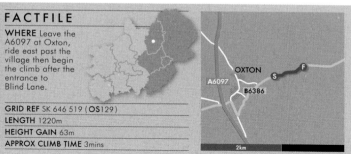

FACTFILE

WHERE Leave the A6097 at Oxton, ride east past the village then begin the climb after the entrance to Blind Lane.

OXTON
A6097
B6386
2km

GRID REF SK 646 519 (OS129)

LENGTH 1220m

HEIGHT GAIN 63m

APPROX CLIMB TIME 3mins

GEORGES HILL

CALVERTON, NOTTINGHAMSHIRE

There is a clutch of small hills forming a barrier between the area north of Nottingham and the village of Calverton, of which this hill is the toughest. Leave Calverton and rise gently, heading south towards the ridge ahead. Passing the national speed limit signs, the slope increases slightly as you make your way towards the first bends. Heading right, the surface changes; the road is now ribbed and does nothing to aid your progress. Next, bending left, things get tougher. The sudden rearing up may take you by surprise, forcing a gulp and an immediate change of gear. Push hard around the left-hand bend and into a gruelling straight to the brow ahead. It's a real grind to the 90-degree corner where you leave tree cover and bend right for the final stretch of climbing. Click up the gears and ride hard all the way to the next corner and the final left-hander where the summit lies.

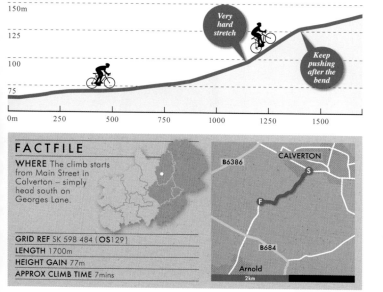

FACTFILE

WHERE The climb starts from Main Street in Calverton – simply head south on Georges Lane.

GRID REF SK 598 484 (OS129)

LENGTH 1700m

HEIGHT GAIN 77m

APPROX CLIMB TIME 7mins

TERRACE HILL

VALE OF BELVOIR, LEICESTERSHIRE

Lying across the borders of Leicestershire, Lincolnshire, and Nottinghamshire, the Vale of Belvoir is an oasis of hilly terrain in a desert of flatland. For those living in Newark, Grantham, or Melton, this is where to head for a tough ride, and of all the hills, Terrace is the best. It satisfies the criteria for a great climb: a quiet road, a couple of twists and turns, varied terrain, and of course a punishing gradient. There's a sense of trepidation as you ride the long approach to the ridge of this ascent, with the road disappearing into the trees ahead. Climbing as soon as you enter the wood, the first few metres start steady and then head straight up; the good surface leads to a steep right-hand bend and the hardest section, before bearing left. The surface – broken in places with new toppings ripped up to expose those below – gradually deteriorates before you reach the peak round to the left.

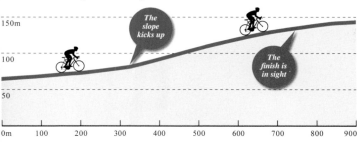

The slope kicks up

The finish is in sight

150m

100

50

0m   100   200   300   400   500   600   700   800   900

FACTFILE

WHERE Follow the road south from the A52 and past the turn to Belvoir. Take the next left to Branston and begin the long approach to Barkestone Wood.

GRID REF SK 798 320 (OS129)

LENGTH 900m

HEIGHT GAIN 76m

APPROX CLIMB TIME 4mins

LINGS HILL

BRANSTON, LEICESTERSHIRE

There are any number of tough little climbs in the Vale of Belvoir, so why have I chosen this one over a handful of other worthy candidates? Well, with Terrace Hill already in the bag, I wanted to find it a companion. I almost went for Harby Hill as it's frequently used for hill climbs; however, Lings Hill has a special place in my heart. The search for adrenaline led me to Terrace, where I found my climbing legs; the craving for more led me here. At 16 years old, on brand new 21mm rubber, I sat at the top of its dead-straight 10% gradient and my perception of speed was to be altered forever. Did I touch the brakes? Unfortunately yes, but you won't need them on the way up. It's a very simple climb, just 500m right up a 10% slope. Pick a suitable gear and nail it. Keep your eyes on the prize – the brow ahead – and fight all the way until you cross it, kinking left to reach the summit.

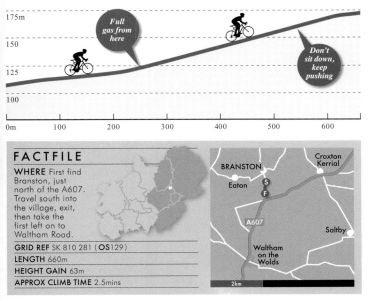

FACTFILE

WHERE First find Branston, just north of the A607. Travel south into the village, exit, then take the first left on to Waltham Road.

GRID REF SK 810 281 (OS129)

LENGTH 660m

HEIGHT GAIN 63m

APPROX CLIMB TIME 2.5mins

BEACON HILL

The Charnwood Forest lies to the north-west of Leicester, although it's more of an open rocky area than an actual forest. Criss-crossed by many roads, it is home to a collection of climbs, the longest of which is this one. The climb from Woodhouse Eaves to the Beacon Hill Country Park entrance serves as a very popular test for local riders. A friend of mine uses it to prep his legs before trips to the mountains, as its steady 8% gradient is a good conditioner for that type of climbing, albeit a little shorter in distance. Leaving the village, the pitch of the slope soon assumes its constant degree of incline. From now to the summit there are slight variations but nothing significant, so pick your gear and settle into a rhythm. Midway, the course gently bends right taking you into the next long straight. This then leads to the kink left and the pronounced brow at the entrance to the Beacon Hill car park.

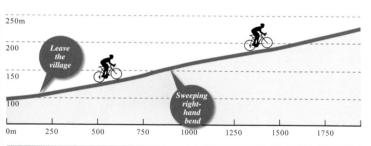

FACTFILE

WHERE The climb starts in Woodhouse Eaves and rises west up the road that forms the northern border of the village.

GRID REF SK 510 145 (OS129)

LENGTH 1950m

HEIGHT GAIN 125m

APPROX CLIMB TIME 6mins

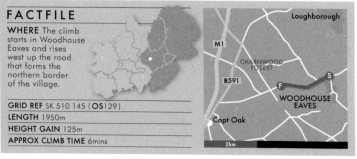

POLLY BOTT'S LANE

MARKFIELD, LEICESTERSHIRE

Polly Bott's Lane has been the venue for the Leicester Forest Cycling Club annual hill climb since 1978, an event that draws many riders from the surrounding counties wanting to test themselves on a truly demanding slope. If a climb becomes home for a long-standing event, then you know you're going to be in for a tough ride. You drop down a few metres from the T-junction to start and cross a brook. After this it begins to climb. It's not the toughest but it's steep enough, picking its way up between Lea Wood and Stoneywell Wood. As the road kinks slightly right and left, the trees begin to fade, and the pitch almost levels as you reach the 90-degree right-hand bend. Once round, you still have a third of the climb left and the slope becomes sharp again. With great views on your left and a line of huge, opulent houses on your right, pull yourself upwards to the brow that lies just shy of the junction.

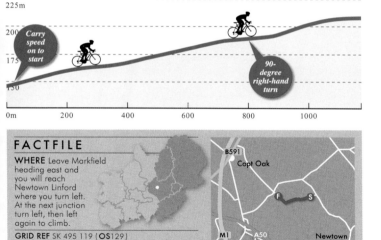

FACTFILE

WHERE Leave Markfield heading east and you will reach Newtown Linford where you turn left. At the next junction turn left, then left again to climb.

GRID REF SK 495 119 (OS129)

LENGTH 1175m

HEIGHT GAIN 65m

APPROX CLIMB TIME 4mins

RATING
1/10

LAUNDE ABBEY

LAUNDE PARK, LEICESTERSHIRE

Without doubt, this is one of the shortest climbs I've ever included in a book – it's a little gem though, and well worth its place in the sun. Passing through Launde Park, an oasis of sheep-manicured, rolling grassland, you turn right in front of the Abbey and face your fate. Free from hedgerows and just wide enough for a single car, the path ahead rises dead straight – a single, neat line of grey bisecting the luscious green hillside. Lined by giant trees either side, try to take some speed on to the slope and get out of the saddle to sprint. The tough gradient kicks in as you pass a road joining from the left and from here on it requires one single, eyeballs-out effort. Hit the remaining 250m of 11% gradient, grip your bars tight, and focus on the brow ahead. By the time you hit it and rumble over the cattle grid to leave the park behind, you should be empty – if not, you need to go back and try harder!

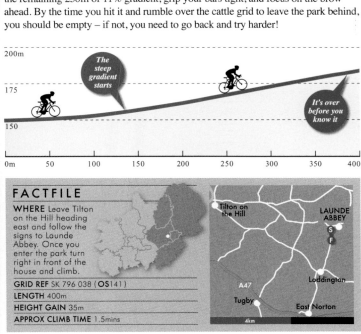

FACTFILE

WHERE Leave Tilton on the Hill heading east and follow the signs to Launde Abbey. Once you enter the park turn right in front of the house and climb.

GRID REF SK 796 038 (**OS**141)

LENGTH 400m

HEIGHT GAIN 35m

APPROX CLIMB TIME 1.5mins

KINGS HILL

UPPINGHAM, RUTLAND

Although not as steep as Rockingham Hill a couple of miles south, Kings Hill is almost twice as long and is a great road to stick into your training loop. The climb starts from the narrowing of the road as a small bridge crosses the brook below. Up ahead you see the hill rise into the distance and the slope gradually begins to build. Leaving Leicestershire and entering Rutland, you approach the first deviation: a 30-degree right-hand bend. As the road gets slightly steeper, you ride up the highlight of the climb: a 20% left-hand hairpin. The gradient eases just before the bend allowing you to gather some speed; you'll have to ride slightly wide of the gutter unless you want to grind to a halt, so watch out for cars behind. Once round you push on up to the next bend, which veers right, and the slope abates allowing you to engage the big ring, attack the summit, and roll into the historic town of Uppingham.

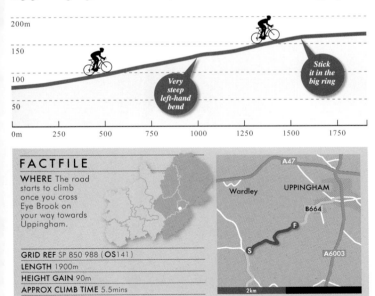

Very steep left-hand bend

Stick it in the big ring

FACTFILE

WHERE The road starts to climb once you cross Eye Brook on your way towards Uppingham.

GRID REF SP 850 988 (OS141)
LENGTH 1900m
HEIGHT GAIN 90m
APPROX CLIMB TIME 5.5mins

ROCKINGHAM HILL

ROCKINGHAM, NORTHAMPTONSHIRE

I've a distinct memory of riding this hill either at the start or the finish of an early season time trial in the early nineties, although my mate Nick says it wasn't on the course. Still, I must have climbed it at some point in an exhausted, cold, and/or wet state, because, scarred for life, I never returned. Until, that is, when I arrived to record it for this book, to see what I'd been afraid of for all those years. It's not a long climb – this is Northamptonshire after all – but it is steep enough to test any rider. You begin as you enter the village from the flat road and then gradually start to rise between the beautifully quaint thatched cottages. It's a stunning little village, but don't dwell – you have a hill to climb. Kinking left, the slope backs off before hitting its maximum of over 10% past one of the entrances to Rockingham Park. Once over this 200m stretch, it gets easier and easier to finish at the roundabout on the edge of Corby.

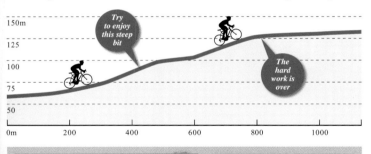

Try to enjoy this steep bit

The hard work is over

150m

125

100

75

50

0m   200   400   600   800   1000

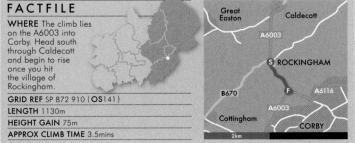

FACTFILE

WHERE The climb lies on the A6003 into Corby. Head south through Caldecott and begin to rise once you hit the village of Rockingham.

GRID REF SP 872 910 (OS141)

LENGTH 1130m

HEIGHT GAIN 75m

APPROX CLIMB TIME 3.5mins

DERBYSHIRE

Snake Pass

Monsal Head

Burbage Moor

Monks' Road

Curbar Edge

Mam Nick

Beeley Moor

Eccles Pike

Carr Lane

Peaslows

Hardwick Hill

Axe Edge

Jaggers Lane

Winnats Pass

Slack Hill

Manners Wood

Riber

Rowsley Bar

Bank Road

Holly Lane

DERBY

CARR LANE

PALTERTON, CHESTERFIELD

Carr Lane had been on my radar for quite a while before I ended up at the base of its slope. Used by the Bolsover and District Cycling Club as the venue for their hill climb, it was one of a few hills in this area I'd never got round to riding. As you approach from Sutton Scarsdale and pass over the M1, the ridge in front looms ominously and the heart rate quickens. From the base you see the route ahead pick its way up to Palterton at the summit; flashes of tarmac are visible here and there between the high hedgerows. The gradient isn't a challenge to start with and it's not until you reach the right–left bends at mid-distance that the slope gets serious. Until this point I'd convinced myself I could tackle it all in the saddle, but these corners forced me out of it briefly. Things become slightly easier for a while and then bending right it kicks up to the top – a stiff finale to a great little climb.

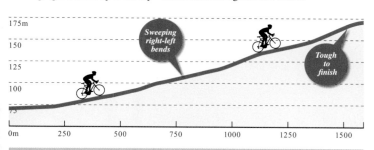

Sweeping right-left bends

Tough to finish

175m
150
125
100
75

0m   250   500   750   1000   1250   1500

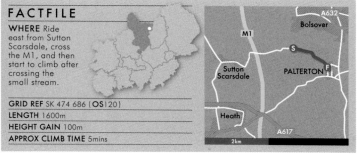

FACTFILE

WHERE Ride east from Sutton Scarsdale, cross the M1, and then start to climb after crossing the small stream.

GRID REF SK 474 686 (OS120)

LENGTH 1600m

HEIGHT GAIN 100m

APPROX CLIMB TIME 5mins

A632
Bolsover
M1
S
Sutton Scarsdale
PALTERTON
F
Heath
A617
2km

HARDWICK HILL

HARDWICK HALL, CHESTERFIELD

Now, to ride this little climb legitimately you'll have to do so in a race. Why? Because the road is one-way, and its ascent involves passing through no entry signs and riding against the traffic. Set in the beautiful grounds of the grand Hardwick Hall, the whole road system runs in one direction: from north to south. So, why include it in the book then? Well, as I go to press, it's the venue for an annual floodlit hill climb up the short yet punishing rise. Organised by the Bolsover and District Cycling Club, this innovative night-time format makes for a fantastic spectacle and is well worth knowing about; hopefully it's an event that will run and run. The ride starts gradually, picks up to the tight left-hand bend, eases back slightly afterwards, and then finishes with more steep stuff to the plateau in front of the Hall – it's over in a flash.

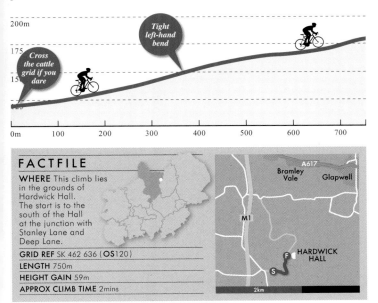

FACTFILE

WHERE This climb lies in the grounds of Hardwick Hall. The start is to the south of the Hall at the junction with Stanley Lane and Deep Lane.

GRID REF SK 462 636 (OS120)

LENGTH 750m

HEIGHT GAIN 59m

APPROX CLIMB TIME 2mins

SLACK HILL

KELSTEDGE, CHESTERFIELD

I've never had a good time on this road – I hate it, I hate it so much, which is the very reason why I had to include it. It is such an unforgiving beast. The first time I came across its cruel slopes was on a youth hostelling weekend, but that time I rode down it. The aim was to see who could achieve the highest speed; I chickened out at 57mph, and to this day I have only been faster once, and that was coming off Mont Ventoux. But to climb Slack Hill is just evil; if bikes had been around in medieval times people would have been forced to ride up it as a form of torture. Approaching from Kelstedge you're faced with the sight of a huge arc of 14% tarmac heading skywards – take all the momentum you can to the base and begin to suffer. There are no corners, no deviation, just struggling. Of course the torment does come to an end – over the brow just past the turning to Beeley. Now, how fast do you dare ride down it?

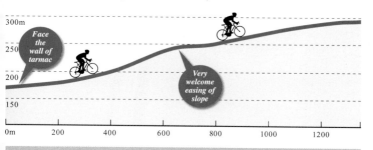

Face the wall of tarmac

Very welcome easing of slope

FACTFILE

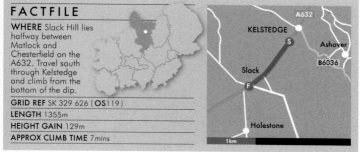

WHERE Slack Hill lies halfway between Matlock and Chesterfield on the A632. Travel south through Kelstedge and climb from the bottom of the dip.

GRID REF SK 329 626 (OS119)

LENGTH 1355m

HEIGHT GAIN 129m

APPROX CLIMB TIME 7mins

RATING
6/10

JAGGERS LANE

KELSTEDGE, CHESTERFIELD

Jaggers Lane sounds nasty, and it is nasty. This rugged sliver of dark tarmac is a wonderfully tough road to seek out and ride. You must begin the climb not on Jaggers Lane, but at the base of the valley – it would be criminal not to, as the first bend away from the brook is fantastic. Rearing up to the left, hitting 20%, it's a killer, and it continues very steep, bending left again before turning right to join Jaggers Lane itself. There's no change in the pitch of the slope; it's proper hard, a real grind. Up ahead there's a brow; focus on that as once you're over it, the complexion of the climb changes. There are a couple of hundred metres of tame gradient, but don't go crazy and click up too many gears because there's more hard climbing to come. Continuing up to and around the right-hand bend, you'll see a give way sign up ahead; this is the target, the carrot to chase. Once past it, you'll reach the T-junction and all will be over.

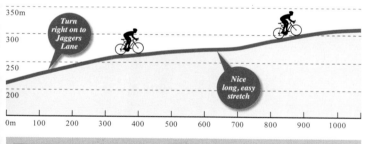

Turn right on to Jaggers Lane

Nice long, easy stretch

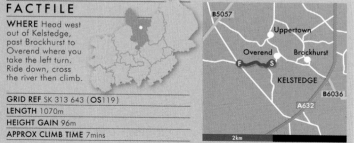

FACTFILE

WHERE Head west out of Kelstedge, past Brockhurst to Overend where you take the left turn. Ride down, cross the river then climb.

B5057

Uppertown

Overend   Brockhurst
F   S

KELSTEDGE

B6036

A632

2km

GRID REF SK 313 643 (OS119)
LENGTH 1070m
HEIGHT GAIN 96m
APPROX CLIMB TIME 7mins

BANK ROAD

MATLOCK

Climbing away from the centre of Matlock, Bank Road is one of the steepest residential roads in England. The venue for multiple National Hill Climb Championships, it turns from the roundabout on the A615 and then ramps up abruptly – a straight line of smooth tarmac between town houses. Beginning around 1-in-6 and getting gradually steeper as it goes, this climb can wear you down like no other. Being an urban road there are numerous drains and parked cars to weave past, as well as markers to focus on, but there's no respite from the relentless slope. The road kinks right towards the top and then left through a steep 1-in-5 section towards a triangular junction. The road opens up here to a large expanse of tarmac; bear right and keep to the far left-hand side where the slope is shallowest, to take as much momentum as possible into the final, gentler section that levels out next to a bus stop.

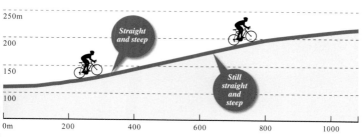

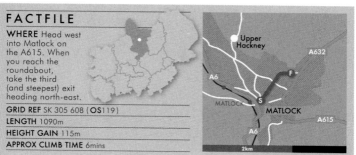

FACTFILE

WHERE Head west into Matlock on the A615. When you reach the roundabout, take the third (and steepest) exit heading north-east.

GRID REF SK 305 608 (OS119)

LENGTH 1090m

HEIGHT GAIN 115m

APPROX CLIMB TIME 6mins

RIBER

MATLOCK

The road up to Riber Castle out of Matlock is a legendary challenge. It starts climbing from where you turn off the A615, just enough to get the heart thumping and the legs burning. This prelude to the main event flattens for 100m, and then, off to the left, there it is – Riber Road – arcing off the main road like a chute, beginning with an insanely steep 1-in-4 left-hander. There's nothing for it but to build some speed, keep wide to the right, hope there's no traffic, and attack the first of five punishing bends. It is merciless all the way, lessening to at best 1-in-6. The second bend sweeps hard right and then left to a double hairpin; the third bend arcs left; the fourth – steeper still – takes you into an impossibly brutal section, its rough, steep surface doing all it can to bring you to a halt. But the end is now in sight in the form of the fifth and final bend, veering left at 1-in-5 to finish at the crown of the road.

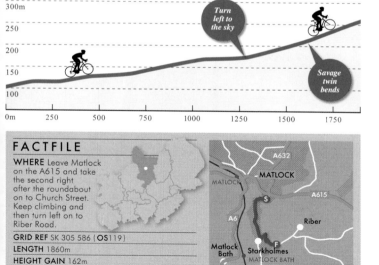

FACTFILE

WHERE Leave Matlock on the A615 and take the second right after the roundabout on to Church Street. Keep climbing and then turn left on to Riber Road.

GRID REF SK 305 586 (OS119)

LENGTH 1860m

HEIGHT GAIN 162m

APPROX CLIMB TIME 8.5mins

HOLLY LANE

AMBERGATE

Holly Lane, or the AHC/3 as it's also known, is a frequently used hill climb course, so you know it's going to be a proper test. I only raced it once, back in 1991, and although not as tough as Riber up the road in Matlock, it certainly hurt. Begin by leaving the A6 in the village; ride past the small stone church, cross the River Derwent, and then the narrow road – framed by low stone walls – bends left and up. Becoming steeper as it rises, it soon hits its maximum gradient as you bend right. Lined out in front of you is a solid stretch of 14% climbing through a tunnel of trees towards the light at the top. As you exit the woods you pass Whitewells Lane on your left and the slope relents a fraction. Keep pushing on, bending gradually right and then straightening once more up to the right–left kink at a solitary farm. It's tough round this corner but eases significantly along the final section to the brow ahead.

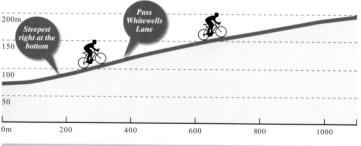

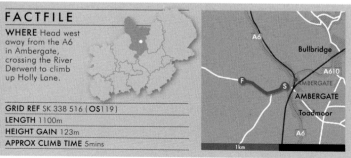

FACTFILE

WHERE Head west away from the A6 in Ambergate, crossing the River Derwent to climb up Holly Lane.

GRID REF SK 338 516 (OS119)

LENGTH 1100m

HEIGHT GAIN 123m

APPROX CLIMB TIME 5mins

ROWSLEY BAR

ROWSLEY

Turn off the A6 into Rowsley and take the first right turn up Chesterfield Lane to begin the climb of Rowsley Bar. Hard from the start, this road's rough surface is dotted with drainage grilles in the gutter and climbs past farm buildings before bending right. The gradient eases as you approach a cottage on your left, after which the climb gets much harder. But here there is a rather fortunate feature to note, as at some point roadworks have left a 30-centimetre-wide strip of super-silky tarmac running the remaining length of the climb. Unwittingly, this provides the optimum and smoothest route to the summit of this otherwise horribly abrasive climb. Two hairpins – 1-in-4 at the apex, first left and then right – are followed very shortly by another very steep left. Your smooth line eventually veers into the centre of the road as you approach the top, forcing you to leave it and complete the last few metres unaided.

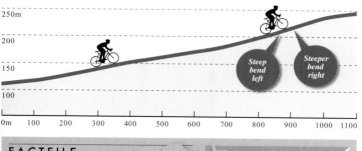

Steep bend left

Steeper bend right

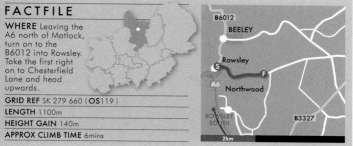

FACTFILE

WHERE Leaving the A6 north of Matlock, turn on to the B6012 into Rowsley. Take the first right on to Chesterfield Lane and head upwards.

GRID REF SK 279 660 (OS119)

LENGTH 1100m

HEIGHT GAIN 140m

APPROX CLIMB TIME 6mins

RATING

4/10

BEELEY MOOR

BEELEY

Beeley Lane up to Beeley Moor is a frequently used hill climb course, not quite steep enough for the pure climbers, but a great road nonetheless. Start from the T-junction outside The Devonshire Arms in the centre of the village. The hardest slopes are in the first third so you can put some extra effort in here, safe in the knowledge that things will get easier further up. Following a noticeable increase in gradient, there's a brief levelling and from here on it's just a degree gentler. You can either take this as the signal to relax a little, or click down a gear and keep pushing as the road meanders in and out of the cover of the woods. Exiting the trees for a final time, press on through the last bend, which takes you on to the exposed moor. The gradient continues to ebb away, but at the same time your exposure to the elements increases, ensuring the long ride to the brow is an effort all the way.

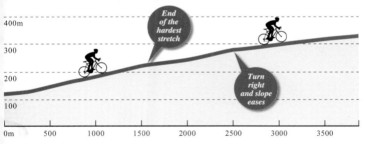

End of the hardest stretch

Turn right and slope eases

FACTFILE

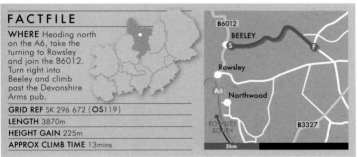

WHERE Heading north on the A6, take the turning to Rowsley and join the B6012. Turn right into Beeley and climb past the Devonshire Arms pub.

GRID REF SK 296 672 (OS119)

LENGTH 3870m

HEIGHT GAIN 225m

APPROX CLIMB TIME 13mins

RATING 6/10

CURBAR EDGE

CURBAR

Turning off the A623, this climb starts very hard – at around 1-in-6. Ending this opening stretch is a steep right-hand bend and then the gradient backs off. Focus on the phone box up ahead in the centre of Curbar village, as this marks roughly one-third of the overall distance. Continuing reasonably gently, you pass through the village and head on to the moor via a sweeping left-hander with a dramatic rocky face of gritstone straight before you. Climb on to the steepest part – a tight right-hand bend followed by a winding stretch of 1-in-6 – where the surface is lumpier, but still good. Once past a couple of car parks on the left, follow the road to a gap in the rocks ahead – a false summit – from where it's not much further to the finish alongside another large car park. A busy spot on weekends, Curbar Edge is a natural multipurpose sports venue, perfect for climbers, walkers, and of course cyclists.

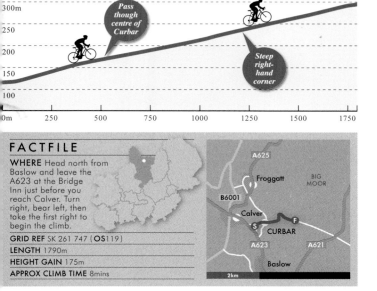

Pass though centre of Curbar

Steep right-hand corner

FACTFILE

WHERE Head north from Baslow and leave the A623 at the Bridge Inn just before you reach Calver. Turn right, bear left, then take the first right to begin the climb.

GRID REF SK 261 747 (OS119)

LENGTH 1790m

HEIGHT GAIN 175m

APPROX CLIMB TIME 8mins

BURBAGE MOOR

HATHERSAGE, HOPE VALLEY

Linking Derbyshire and Yorkshire, the climb out of Hathersage should not be underestimated. To begin, make your way south on the A6187 and turn left on to School Lane. The road levels outside the school and you start the climb proper from here. Heading up and round to the right, you pass The Scotsmans Pack pub and wind through some houses. The gradient increases as you pass the last house and bend to the left. After backing off a pinch, the road then makes its way round to the right and ramps up steeper and steeper towards a left-hand bend. Here the hard climbing ends for a while and up ahead you see the exposed rock face, which on any day will be dotted with brightly clad climbers. Ride up to the base, level out, and then bank right into the finale. A solid slog, punctuated only by a couple of sets of rumble strips – the second set coming just before the peak of the road, where the gradient disappears.

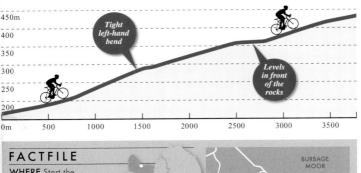

Tight left-hand bend

Levels in front of the rocks

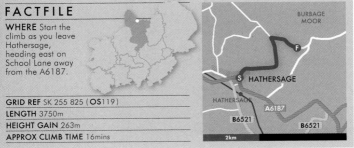

FACTFILE

WHERE Start the climb as you leave Hathersage, heading east on School Lane away from the A6187.

GRID REF SK 255 825 (OS119)	
LENGTH 3750m	
HEIGHT GAIN 263m	
APPROX CLIMB TIME 16mins	

RATING
7/10

MANNERS WOOD

BAKEWELL

No visit to Bakewell is complete without purchasing one of its famous tarts, but in order to enjoy it guilt-free you'll have to take in some hills – so where better to start than here? Begin at the congested junction on the A619 and rise up through the houses. The slope is nice and steady to begin with and soon kinks left to face the car park for the Monsal Trail. At this point, take the right-hand turn and head towards the golf club. Rising past the entrance, the gradient is stiffer, and at the time of writing the surface was pitted and broken. Upon reaching a brilliant hairpin, you turn back on yourself and continue to climb under a covering of trees next to a crumbling stone wall, seemingly only held together by a film of luscious moss. The pitch of the narrow slope varies as you rise high above Bakewell, leading you to a left-hand bend and the final, agonising 500m to the point where you can climb no further.

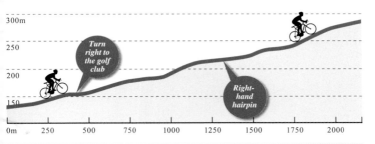

Turn right to the golf club

Right-hand hairpin

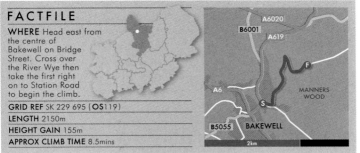

FACTFILE

WHERE Head east from the centre of Bakewell on Bridge Street. Cross over the River Wye then take the first right on to Station Road to begin the climb.

GRID REF SK 229 695 (OS119)

LENGTH 2150m

HEIGHT GAIN 155m

APPROX CLIMB TIME 8.5mins

MONSAL HEAD

ASHFORD IN THE WATER, BAKEWELL

This perfect arc of smooth tarmac takes you from the bank of the River Wye to an amphitheatre-like finish in front of the inn at the top. It's not the steepest climb, having a maximum gradient of just 1-in-6, and far from the longest, so Monsal Head is an unremarkable ascent compared to some. But nonetheless it's a favourite hill climb course, for which the record holder is still the great Malcolm Elliott. Set in 1981, his 1 minute 14.2 seconds has withstood all challenges, so keep this in mind when you set your computer at the bottom. As you start, look carefully and you will see 6 inches of repaired road in the left gutter. This super-smooth surface will aid your search for speed over the opening section. Since the gradient is steady the whole way, with no twists and turns, you have nothing to distract you from your task – force the pedals, round the corner, and check your time: have you beaten the record?

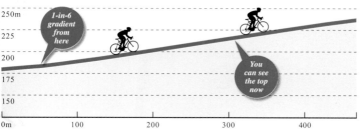

FACTFILE

WHERE Leave the A6020 at Ashford in the Water and take the B6465 north. Follow this to Monsal Head, turn left, descend, and then turn round to climb back up.

GRID REF SK 184 715 (OS119)

LENGTH 470m

HEIGHT GAIN 57m

APPROX CLIMB TIME 2.5mins

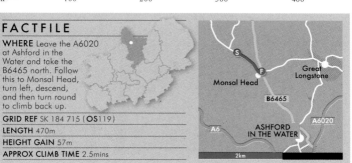

WINNATS PASS

For sheer drama, nothing matches Winnats Pass – a winding road twisting through a natural cleft, surrounded by towering, grass-covered limestone pinnacles. Leaving the village of Castleton on the A6187, take a left and begin. The sign says 1-in-5 and so it is, all the way to the top, passing car parks and tourist sites and over what may be the steepest cattle grid in England, where you enter the amazing gorge. The grassy banks either side are perfectly pruned and form a natural 'V', with you pedalling right in the centre. The silky-smooth surface sweeps gently right before winding slightly and turning left to the summit. The banks fade with every grinding pedal stroke and the sky opens up, but the slope never eases, not for a moment. For many years, this climb was the cornerstone of the now defunct Tour of the Peak cycle race. To think it was climbed after almost 145 kilometres of hard racing defies belief.

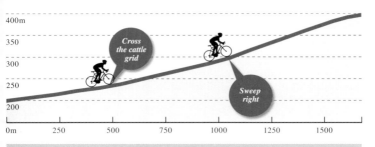

FACTFILE

WHERE Head west out of Castleton on the A6187. As the road bends right, take the route straight ahead up into the gorge.

GRID REF SK 129 828 (OS119)

LENGTH 1680m

HEIGHT GAIN 198m

APPROX CLIMB TIME 9mins

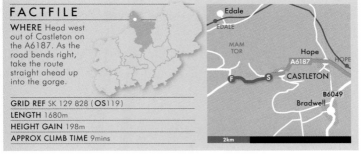

MAM NICK

BARBER BOOTH, EDALE

Mam Nick is a marvellous snaking road that climbs up out of Edale to Rushup Edge. It's tough, but a good few degrees kinder than the infamous Winnats Pass on the other side of the ridge. Beginning just outside the village of Barber Booth, the gradient hits 1-in-6 straight away as you cross a small bridge, but lasts only a short distance before easing off. Following the first left bend it's easier still, but not for long: more tough stuff is on its way. Mam Tor, translating as 'Heights of the Mother', looms way above you, watching your progress as the road gets steeper, weaving left and right like water flowing between rocks in a stream. As you enter the last few bends, it appears as if a giant blanket of green felt has been laid over the land, smoothing out all the rocks and bumps. Keep pushing through this surreal Tellytubbies-like scenery to finish where the road cuts its way through the gap in the ridge.

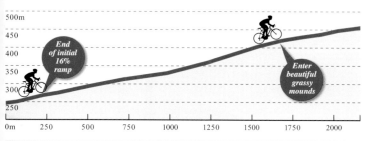

End of initial 16% ramp

Enter beautiful grassy mounds

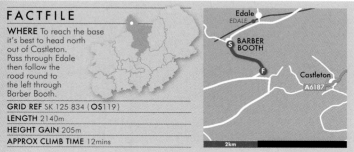

FACTFILE

WHERE To reach the base it's best to head north out of Castleton. Pass through Edale then follow the road round to the left through Barber Booth.

GRID REF SK 125 834 (OS119)

LENGTH 2140m

HEIGHT GAIN 205m

APPROX CLIMB TIME 12mins

RATING
5/10

SNAKE PASS

GLOSSOP

The Snake Pass would certainly be one of Britain's greatest cycling climbs if it weren't for the traffic. Its six kilometres of perfectly pitched tarmac, winding through beautiful moorland, is simply ruined by the volume and proximity of the ever-flowing vehicles. For this reason I refused to include it in either of my first two books on Britain's greatest cycling climbs, but I've decided to admit it for entry to this volume because when quiet, it's just so rewarding to ride. Rising out of Glossop you soon hit the lower 14% slopes where the transition from gentle climbing to the more substantial gradient isn't as sharp as it at first appears. The tough start lasts only to the first right-hand bend and from then on the climb is set on an ideal gradient that literally 'snakes' up across the barren landscape. The slope is all but uniform until you approach the expansive plateau at the summit where it eases to finish in the fantastic solitude of the High Peak.

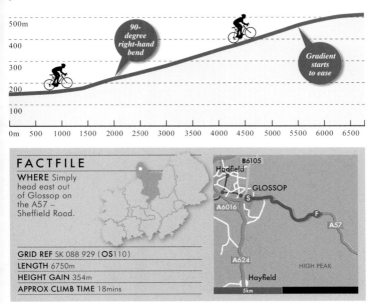

500m
400
300
200
100

0m 500 1000 1500 2000 2500 3000 3500 4000 4500 5000 5500 6000 6500

90-degree right-hand bend

Gradient starts to ease

FACTFILE

WHERE Simply head east out of Glossop on the A57 – Sheffield Road.

B6105
Hadfield
GLOSSOP
A6016
A57
A624
HIGH PEAK
Hayfield
5km

GRID REF SK 088 929 (**OS**110)

LENGTH 6750m

HEIGHT GAIN 354m

APPROX CLIMB TIME 18mins

MONKS' ROAD

CHARLESWORTH

The most obvious route to take if you're heading south out of Glossop is the tough but fairly busy Chunal Hill – the A624. If you travel a couple of kilometres west though, you'll arrive in the village of Charlesworth and from here you can tackle the harder and much quieter Monks' Road. Leaving Town Lane, you turn south on to Chapel Brow and right away it's a struggle out of the village. Past the last house a huge stone wall bordering the chapel grounds begins on the right. This offers excellent shelter from any wind that may be coming from the west, so you may be very thankful for it. Leaving the wall behind, the severity of the slope increases up to a fake brow, which marks the end of the steep stuff and ushers in a much kinder challenge. From here on, the road gradually bends to the right and is exposed all the way up to one final kick – one last hurrah before it bends right and drops down.

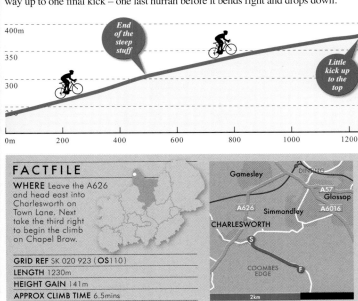

FACTFILE

WHERE Leave the A626 and head east into Charlesworth on Town Lane. Next take the third right to begin the climb on Chapel Brow.

GRID REF SK 020 923 (**OS**110)

LENGTH 1230m

HEIGHT GAIN 141m

APPROX CLIMB TIME 6.5mins

RATING
6/10

ECCLES PIKE

CHAPEL-EN-LE-FRITH

The name pike means 'pointed hill', and there are two ways up to this particular apex: one from the west, and this one from the east. I preferred this side, but of course feel free to ride them both and make your own mind up. Leaving Chapel-en-le-Frith on either Crossings Road or Eccles Road, you'll reach the base where the two meet and the push towards the point at the top of the hill begins. Past the last of the houses there's some solid climbing to get stuck into, followed by a welcome rest before the proper work starts. As the trees clear, you'll see the pike on the horizon ahead – first over to your left, and then, as you climb closer, to your right. The higher slopes are framed by scrubby grassland and offer fantastic views out over the Combs Reservoir as you push on to the summit, which is now square ahead, waiting for you to cross; drop down the other side, and then head back up again.

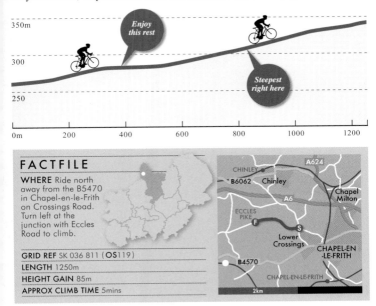

Enjoy this rest

Steepest right here

350m

300

250

0m   200   400   600   800   1000   1200

FACTFILE

WHERE Ride north away from the B5470 in Chapel-en-le-Frith on Crossings Road. Turn left at the junction with Eccles Road to climb.

GRID REF SK 036 811 (OS119)

LENGTH 1250m

HEIGHT GAIN 85m

APPROX CLIMB TIME 5mins

CHINLEY

A624

B6062 Chinley

A6

Chapel Milton

ECCLES PIKE
F

Lower Crossings

S
CHAPEL-EN-LE-FRITH

B4570

CHAPEL-EN-LE-FRITH

2km

RATING
4/10

PEASLOWS

CHAPEL-EN-LE-FRITH

Leaving the tiny village of Blackbrook, just off the A6 east of Chapel-en-le-Frith, Peaslows climbs over the ridge to Sparrowpit and into the Peak District National Park. A gradual climb, it's neither too steep nor too shallow. It begins once past a dead end sign over the brook and climbs into a light cover of tall trees. Its well-maintained surface has a rough topping, but is free of potholes. Once out from under the canopy of trees, you pass a house on the left, where the scenery opens up. Bordered with stone walls and now dead straight, the rest of the climb lies before you with no landmarks to aim for but the top, which seems an awfully long way. It's a solid, constant, 1-in-10 drag, with nowhere to recover and no opportunity to alter your pace, making it a slog and grind to the visible summit (marked on the map as a reservoir). But persevere – on the other side is a lovely steep descent to hurtle down.

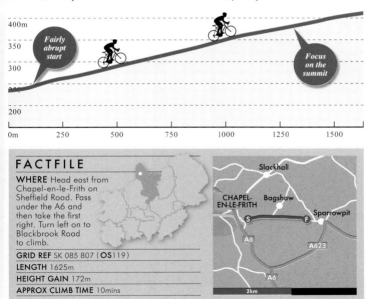

- *Fairly abrupt start*
- *Focus on the summit*

0m	250	500	750	1000	1250	1500

400m
350
300
200

FACTFILE

WHERE Head east from Chapel-en-le-Frith on Sheffield Road. Pass under the A6 and then take the first right. Turn left on to Blackbrook Road to climb.

GRID REF SK 085 807 (**OS**119)

LENGTH 1625m

HEIGHT GAIN 172m

APPROX CLIMB TIME 10mins

Slackhall

CHAPEL-EN-LE-FRITH   Bagshaw
S   F Sparrowpit

A6   A623

A6

2km

AXE EDGE

BUXTON

Not quite as harsh as its name suggests, Axe Edge is nonetheless a solid climb, which can be a real morale breaker in the wrong conditions. The ascent begins somewhere in the busy centre of Buxton, but I chose to measure my distance from the final set of traffic lights at the junction with the B5059. Rising gently away from town, a little steeper past a garage and the junction for the A54, you are soon free of habitation and heading towards the Edge. The whole climb is now lined out in front of you – a constant, exposed gradient stretching up and round the gritstone mound. As you enter the Peak District National Park, choose your gear and settle into a comfortable rhythm to drive you along the smooth but attritional surface. As it approaches a fake summit, the road is lined with a chequered Armco barrier; here you drop a little, so shift up and power to the second brow and the true summit.

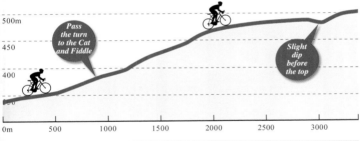

Pass the turn to the Cat and Fiddle

Slight dip before the top

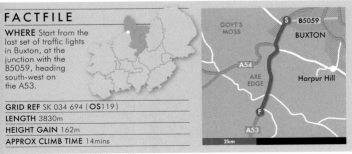

FACTFILE

WHERE Start from the last set of traffic lights in Buxton, at the junction with the B5059, heading south-west on the A53.

GRID REF SK 034 694 (**OS**119)

LENGTH 3830m

HEIGHT GAIN 162m

APPROX CLIMB TIME 14mins

WEST
MIDLANDS
PART ONE

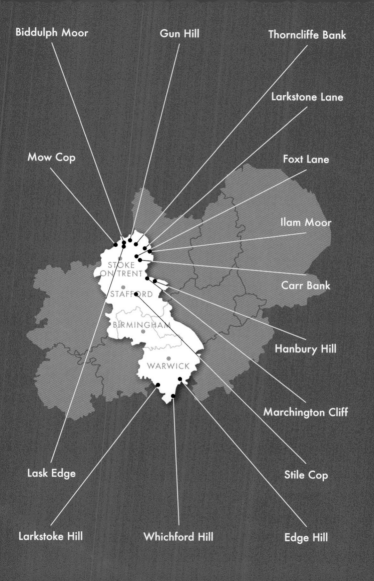

Biddulph Moor

Gun Hill

Thorncliffe Bank

Larkstone Lane

Mow Cop

Foxt Lane

Ilam Moor

Carr Bank

Hanbury Hill

Marchington Cliff

Lask Edge

Stile Cop

Larkstoke Hill

Whichford Hill

Edge Hill

STOKE
ON TRENT

STAFFORD

BIRMINGHAM

WARWICK

GUN HILL

LEEK, STAFFORDSHIRE

You begin the climb up Gun Hill outside The Lazy Trout in the village of Meerbrook. The slope is gentle at first, bending slightly left then later right as you pull away from the scattered houses and head into the cover of trees. After this kink the gradient starts to bite and it becomes a completely different climb. It's steep now and the surface is rough and broken. This twinset of obstacles will seriously slow your pace. Exiting the shade of the trees, the road begins to step its way towards the exposed summit, first hard, then easing, then hard again; each step up tougher than the one before, until you reach a large sweeping right-hand bend. This marks the beginning of the end of the steep stuff. In a race, this is where the strong riders would give it their all, consolidating any advantage they might have over those distanced on the lower slopes. Switch down a gear and build your momentum to claim the finish at the brow.

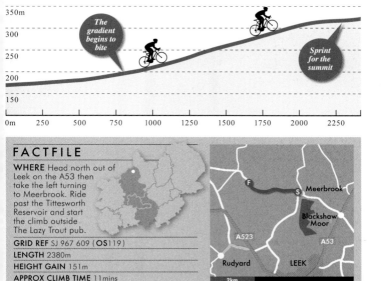

The gradient begins to bite

Sprint for the summit

FACTFILE

WHERE Head north out of Leek on the A53 then take the left turning to Meerbrook. Ride past the Tittesworth Reservoir and start the climb outside The Lazy Trout pub.

GRID REF SJ 967 609 (OS119)

LENGTH 2380m

HEIGHT GAIN 151m

APPROX CLIMB TIME 11mins

THORNCLIFFE BANK

THORNCLIFFE, STAFFORDSHIRE

Often overlooked in favour of its more popular neighbour on the opposite side of the A53, Gun Hill, this climb may be a little shorter, but it's certainly a few degrees tougher. The hard work begins as you enter Thorncliffe, heading east towards the ridge and the border of the Peak District. Passing an old phone box, the slope kicks up violently and kinks round to the right. This first strength-sapping ramp delivers you to a mini-plateau in front of some farm buildings. Here you can compose yourself before getting stuck back into more of the steep stuff. With the glorious views out over the valley on your left, you grind up to a brace of bends, left then right as the gradient momentarily vanishes once more. From here on it's hard work to the top; on and on you climb, over a couple of false brows, until you finally reach the junction with Morridgeside and the entrance to the Peak District National Park.

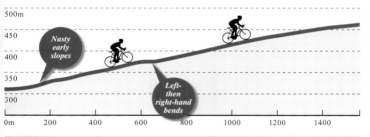

Nasty early slopes

Left-then right-hand bends

FACTFILE

WHERE Leave the A53 north of Leek and follow it into Thorncliffe. Begin the climb as you exit the village on Thorncliffe Bank.

GRID REF SK 028 595 (OS119)

LENGTH 1560m

HEIGHT GAIN 150m

APPROX CLIMB TIME 7mins

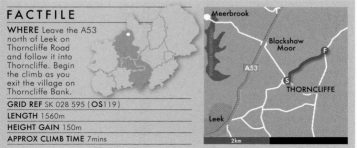

RATING
6/10

LARKSTONE LANE

GRINDON, STAFFORDSHIRE

In a quiet corner of the Peak District, far from the madding crowds surrounding Matlock and Buxton, lies the Manifold Valley. Of the number of ways in and out of the gorge, Larkstone Lane is the toughest. Coming out of Grindon there is a very nasty, rough descent, so take care. Cross a small stone bridge and follow the road as it bends right, climbing gently towards the initial hairpin. Here's where the hard work begins – 25% at the apex, it delivers you into a gruelling 20% stretch before doubling back on itself at the next horribly steep corner. The road, now edged by a typical drystone wall, climbs gently for a while before ramping up again as the surface slowly deteriorates. Before long you're left with just a few inches of clean tarmac either side of the grass and rubble that cover the crown, and then you dip down before the final rise to the summit at the junction with Ashbourne Lane.

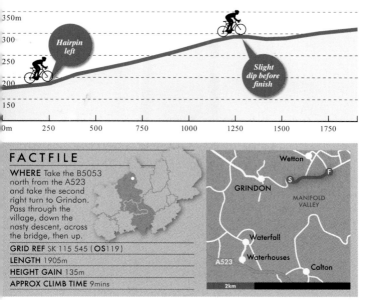

FACTFILE

WHERE Take the B5053 north from the A523 and take the second right turn to Grindon. Pass through the village, down the nasty descent, across the bridge, then up.

GRID REF SK 115 545 (OS119)

LENGTH 1905m

HEIGHT GAIN 135m

APPROX CLIMB TIME 9mins

ILAM MOOR

ILAM, STAFFORDSHIRE

Starting from the centre of the picturesque village of Ilam at the base of the giant, gothic-style stone obelisk, this long, tough climb heads north up on to the moor. The initial slopes are very demanding – easily 15% – so don't go crazy, as you still have a long way to ride. Kinking right past a few houses, the slope soon fades to a welcome levelling where you can glance right to admire the rocky peaks of Bunster Hill. After passing a solitary house, the easy climbing ends and the road twists up between high stone walls into a small wood. Steep and steeper still through the corners, it's a joy to ride as you bend left and right to a pronounced brow. From here the road's course deviates slightly eastwards, and for the rest of its length the gradient is very relaxed. As you close in on the summit, you can build up some speed to finish at pace, adjacent to the track running down to Musden Grange Farm.

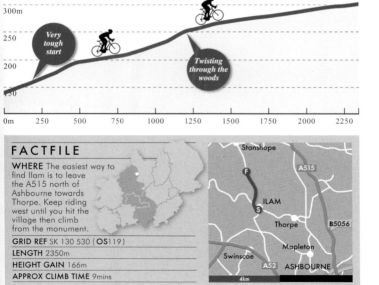

FACTFILE

WHERE The easiest way to find Ilam is to leave the A515 north of Ashbourne towards Thorpe. Keep riding west until you hit the village then climb from the monument.

GRID REF SK 130 530 (OS119)

LENGTH 2350m

HEIGHT GAIN 166m

APPROX CLIMB TIME 9mins

RATING
5/10

BIDDULPH MOOR

BIDDULPH MOOR, STAFFORDSHIRE

It's a long old slog from the sheltered base in the valley to the windy top of Biddulph Moor and it's a climb of two distinct halves. The slope rises gently at first and on my own ascent I was confident I'd be able to complete it in the saddle – no such luck. Spinning comfortably, and with plenty of sprockets to spare, half of me was content with the effort required, but the other half of me craved a stiffer test. A stiffer test is what I got. The road is much wider than any of the other climbs up this ridge, and as it begins to twist and turn the gradient begins to bite. Snaking upwards from now on, this climb is a struggle. Lying in the shadow of the tall, grassy bank on your left, the higher you rise, the grander the views over your shoulder; in fact I would go as far as to encourage you to stop so that you can soak it all in before you reach the very top past the final couple of bends.

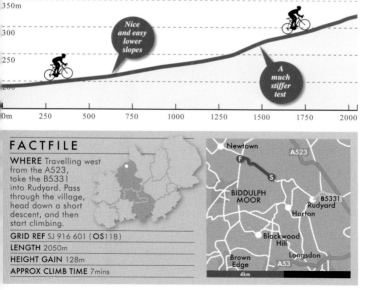

Nice and easy lower slopes

A much stiffer test

FACTFILE

WHERE Travelling west from the A523, take the B5331 into Rudyard. Pass through the village, head down a short descent, and then start climbing.

GRID REF SJ 916 601 (OS118)

LENGTH 2050m

HEIGHT GAIN 128m

APPROX CLIMB TIME 7mins

LASK EDGE

BIDDULPH MOOR, STAFFORDSHIRE

I couldn't leave Biddulph Moor without bagging a second climb, and with quite a few to choose from it was hard to come to a decision. But thanks to its twists and turns on the savage lower slopes, this climb took the honours, even though its neighbour, Park House Lane, is possibly a touch steeper in places. Begin the climb from the ford; I'd never advise riding through one, though, so use the footbridge. From here it kicks up right away and before long will have you breathing out of your ears. Bending through a collection of farm buildings, a very steep right-hand bend then kinks left and snakes upwards on a slope that must be close to 20%. After this demanding stretch, the gradient thankfully relaxes for a couple of hundred metres as you approach the junction with Park House Lane. After the two roads meet, it's time to toil some more for the finish at the T-junction on top of the moor.

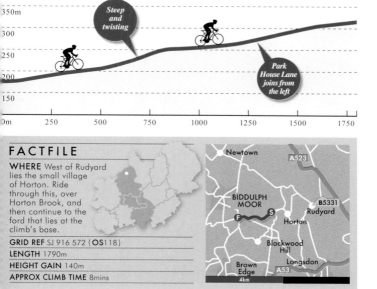

Steep and twisting

Park House Lane joins from the left

350m
300
250
200
150
0m   250   500   750   1000   1250   1500   1750

FACTFILE

WHERE West of Rudyard lies the small village of Horton. Ride through this, over Horton Brook, and then continue to the ford that lies at the climb's base.

GRID REF SJ 916 572 (**OS**118)

LENGTH 1790m

HEIGHT GAIN 140m

APPROX CLIMB TIME 8mins

Newtown

A523

BIDDULPH MOOR

B5331

Rudyard

Horton

Blackwood Hill

Brown Edge

Longsdon

A53

4km

MOW COP

STOKE-ON-TRENT, STAFFORDSHIRE

Mention Mow Cop to cyclists in the West Midlands and their faces may well turn pale with fear. The climb's final section is so steep that during sportives, photographers position themselves here just to capture riders as they topple sideways. To fully test your legs, begin from the railway crossing at its base. Climbing gently past a few houses, the road gets steeper as you bend right then left, then steeper still up to a fake brow. The surface is lumpy and rough but overall in good condition. Over this brow, the gradient lessens. Pass a right turn and aim straight ahead at the wall of tarmac that you have to scale next. Rising dead straight now, and increasingly steeper, your destiny awaits in the form of a 25% 200-metre ramp. Engage your lowest gear, get out of the saddle, and force your pedals past the Cheshire View inn, the proximity of which dramatically emphasises the breathtaking gradient.

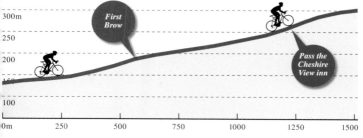

First Brow

Pass the Cheshire View inn

300m
250
200
100
0m   250   500   750   1000   1250   1500

FACTFILE

WHERE Heading north from Kidsgrove on the A34, take the first right out of Scholar Green. Take the second right across the rail tracks to climb.

GRID REF SJ 856 572 (**OS**118)

LENGTH 1505m

HEIGHT GAIN 170m

APPROX CLIMB TIME 8mins

A34
Scholar Green
Mount Pleasant
MOW COP
S
F
2km

FOXT LANE

FROGHALL, STAFFORDSHIRE

All roads from Froghall, in all directions, head upwards. You have the impossibly grim and busy 16% slopes of the A52; the equally steep yet not quite as congested B5053 into Ipstones; and this climb, through the village of Foxt. Leaving the main road, you pass the picturesque surroundings of some parkland and waterworks before settling into your task. It's steep right away – well over 10% – and a real challenge until the slope backs off on the approach to the first houses of Foxt. Ahead you see the village sign and then, as you pass a group of buildings, the road bends tight right and immediately left to ease in front of a short line of cottages. Now comes another bend and more hard work, this time left; it's steep to a brow, bends right, and then you ride into the heart of the village. Navigate through and out the other side to continue to the summit, 100m shy of the junction with Shaw-Wall Lane.

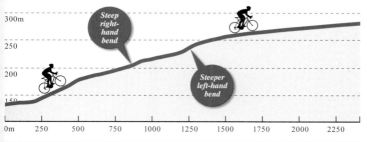

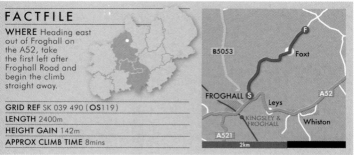

FACTFILE

WHERE Heading east out of Froghall on the A52, take the first left after Froghall Road and begin the climb straight away.

GRID REF SK 039 490 (OS119)

LENGTH 2400m

HEIGHT GAIN 142m

APPROX CLIMB TIME 8mins

RATING
7/10

CARR BANK

OAKAMOOR, STAFFORDSHIRE

I found myself in this corner of Staffordshire – within earshot of the screams coming from the nearby Alton Towers theme park – to try out Star Bank, up the B4517. I was underwhelmed upon reaching the top, though, so I placed it on the 'maybe' list before ultimately moving it to the trash bin after riding Carr Bank. This one's a belter. Start from the B4517 in the centre of Oakamoor, ride past the pub, over the stream, and get pedalling as it kicks up viciously through the houses. It's almost 20% as it kinks left past the church, and then right to head out of the village. Once free of the houses, the slope eases and you head through farmland to a 90-degree left-hand bend, which is followed shortly after by a right. Picking your way past a few trees into a wood, the slope is still stiff in places but nowhere near as hard as it was down at the bottom. The final stretch is easier still, taking you to the summit just round a final left-hand bend.

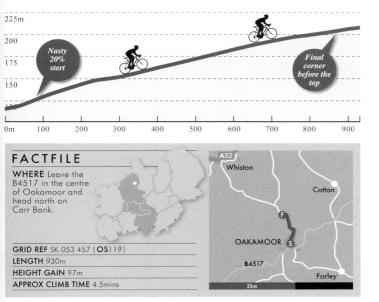

FACTFILE

WHERE Leave the B4517 in the centre of Oakamoor and head north on Carr Bank.

GRID REF SK 053 457 (OS119)

LENGTH 930m

HEIGHT GAIN 97m

APPROX CLIMB TIME 4.5mins

MARCHINGTON CLIFF

MARCHINGTON, STAFFORDSHIRE

Between Hanbury in the east and Gorsty Hill in the west, there are six paths you can choose from to climb up this small ridge to the north-west of Burton upon Trent. Of these six, I've picked two: firstly this hill, Marchington Cliff, and secondly Hanbury Hill, which you will find on page 110. Travelling south from the B5017, you rise a few metres to be met by the twin warnings of a curvaceous road and a 12% gradient. With the promise of fun ahead, the slope rears up and sweeps around the first steep bend in front of a couple of houses. Curving left, you then line up for a sharper bend, this time right and marked with garish direction arrows. It is here that the gradient hits its maximum of 12%, so be ready for the fight and make sure you're in a suitable gear. Now through the worst, the climb peters out at the brow where the road bends left to meet the route that lines the top of the ridge.

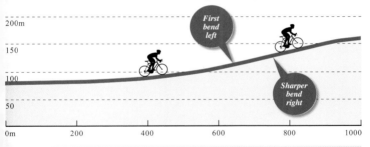

FACTFILE

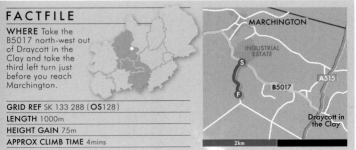

WHERE Take the B5017 north-west out of Draycott in the Clay and take the third left turn just before you reach Marchington.

GRID REF SK 133 288 (OS128)

LENGTH 1000m

HEIGHT GAIN 75m

APPROX CLIMB TIME 4mins

RATING 2/10

HANBURY HILL

HANBURY, STAFFORDSHIRE

I chose two climbs from the collection of hills that make their way up this ridge: Marchington Cliff (see page 109) and Hanbury Hill. Out of these two, I reckon Hanbury is the toughest. You may not think so at first, but believe me – this climb bites towards the top. Leaving Coton Lane, you set off between high hedgerows with your task laid bare in front of you. As the hedgerows recede, the road begins to squirm right then left and the gradient steps up. It's still not tough, not by any stretch of the imagination, but it soon will be. As the bends end, the road ramps up and narrows – now it's hard, now it will hurt. The high hedgerows return; this time they tower above you on the right with woodland on your left, creating a canyon of green. Push the gear over, heave yourself up, and keep fighting. It may be steep but it's soon over, and before long you'll be bending left to roll into Hanbury village.

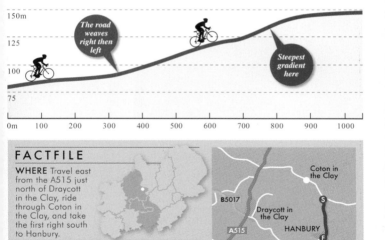

FACTFILE

WHERE Travel east from the A515 just north of Draycott in the Clay, ride through Coton in the Clay, and take the first right south to Hanbury.

GRID REF SK 173 278 (**OS**128)

LENGTH 1050m

HEIGHT GAIN 67m

APPROX CLIMB TIME 3mins

STILE COP

RUGELEY, STAFFORDSHIRE

This climb heads up and away from Rugeley into Regent's Wood at the lower end of Cannock Chase – a large area of country park between Cannock and Stafford. There are a few roads that cross the park but in my opinion this route, just south of the A460, is the best climb. With so little on offer in the way of tough gradient in such a heavily populated area, it's also a favourite with the locals. Leave the A460 just south of Rugeley and ease yourself into the gentle lower slopes as you see the road disappear into the woods ahead. About halfway up, the task becomes distinctly harder, but it's only 600m to the summit so get out of the saddle and attack it. From the picnic area on your left it's almost a dead-straight line to the top, until the consistently challenging slope kinks left to finish at the Stile Cop car park.

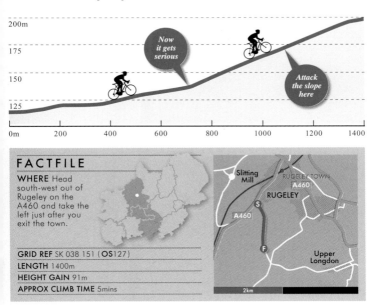

FACTFILE

WHERE Head south-west out of Rugeley on the A460 and take the left just after you exit the town.

GRID REF SK 038 151 (OS127)

LENGTH 1400m

HEIGHT GAIN 91m

APPROX CLIMB TIME 5mins

LARKSTOKE HILL

ILMINGTON, WARWICKSHIRE

This climb was recommended by a Twitter follower, so I just had to see it in the flesh. First of all I double-checked the Landranger map to see if it had the essential gradient arrow – it did. This was going to be fun. On the approach from Ilmington you catch sight of the road stepping up the ridge, and sure enough it looks pretty demanding as it disappears over the top. Hard straight away, it bends slightly right; there's some respite here but before long it's steep again. As you veer right a brow appears, along with the hope that the pain will be short-lived; but to my surprise, this was not the top. Having never ridden it before, I truly expected this to be the summit, but once over I realised I wasn't even half way. Thankfully there's a slight dip before the final ascent, which, although not quite as steep as before, leads you up and up and up towards a small cluster of radio masts and phone transmitters – these mark the final summit.

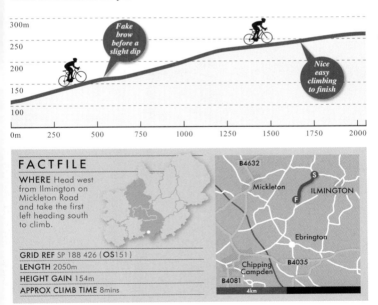

Fake brow before a slight dip

Nice easy climbing to finish

FACTFILE

WHERE Head west from Ilmington on Mickleton Road and take the first left heading south to climb.

GRID REF SP 188 426 (**OS**151)	
LENGTH 2050m	
HEIGHT GAIN 154m	
APPROX CLIMB TIME 8mins	

B4632
Mickleton
ILMINGTON
Ebrington
Chipping Campden
B4035
B4081
4km

RATING
3/10

WHICHFORD HILL

WHICHFORD, WARWICKSHIRE

Whichford lies at the very southern tip of Warwickshire and this climb rises up and out of the village to the border with Oxfordshire and the South-East. There aren't many congested contours on the map around here, so any decent climb is treasured. Before I chose Whichford Hill, I did consider the two stiff ascents that head straight out of Long Compton; however, I settled on this one as it's that bit longer. Start from the centre of the village adjacent to the large square of grass that sits at its heart. The early slopes are a tough 10% for a couple of hundred metres, but then they fade away. For close to a kilometre after this the climbing is extremely sedate, until you reach the last third where the steep stuff returns. Not quite as demanding here as on the slopes at the base, it's still enough to have you out of the saddle to fight all the way to the summit, which lies at the junction.

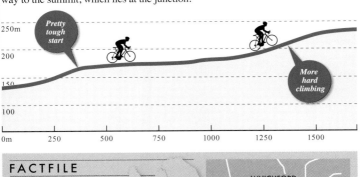

Pretty tough start

More hard climbing

250m

200

150

100

0m   250   500   750   1000   1250   1500

FACTFILE

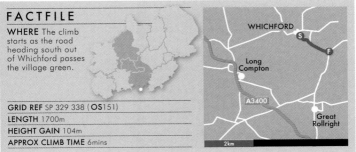

WHERE The climb starts as the road heading south out of Whichford passes the village green.

WHICHFORD
S
F
Long Compton
A3400
Great Rollright
2km

GRID REF SP 329 338 (**OS**151)

LENGTH 1700m

HEIGHT GAIN 104m

APPROX CLIMB TIME 6mins

EDGE HILL

Edge Hill dominates the skyline to the north-west of Banbury – a raised peninsula jutting up from the northern edge of the Cotswolds. Of the number of ways up the ridge, I've chosen the B4086 through Knowle Wood. Although not as tough or as steep as the A422 (Sun Rising Hill) to its west, it's a far nicer ride than the very busy A-road. Start the climb at the junction with Gosport Lane and head up towards the ridge. You've a gentle prelude as the road bends smoothly upwards and around to the right. Through the corner your legs will be tested, as the road straightens and heads up towards the woods. Once into the protection of the trees, the gradient starts to bite. The road is wide and well surfaced and, although never drastically steep, is certainly a slog and, if anything, gets that little bit steeper as you approach the summit at the T-junction. From here you can head down into the beautiful Cotswolds.

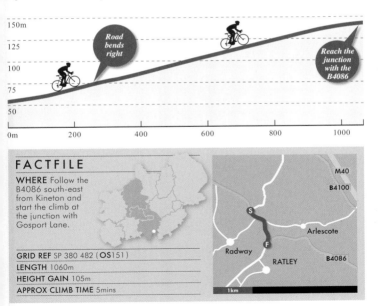

FACTFILE

WHERE Follow the B4086 south-east from Kineton and start the climb at the junction with Gosport Lane.

GRID REF SP 380 482 (OS151)

LENGTH 1060m

HEIGHT GAIN 105m

APPROX CLIMB TIME 5mins

WEST MIDLANDS PART ONE

WEST MIDLANDS
PART TWO

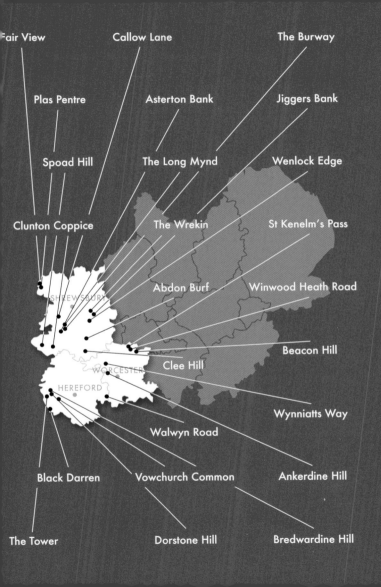

Fair View

Callow Lane

The Burway

Plas Pentre

Asterton Bank

Jiggers Bank

Spoad Hill

The Long Mynd

Wenlock Edge

Clunton Coppice

The Wrekin

St Kenelm's Pass

SHREWSBURY

Abdon Burf

Winwood Heath Road

WORCESTER

Clee Hill

Beacon Hill

HEREFORD

Wynniatts Way

Walwyn Road

Black Darren

Vowchurch Common

Ankerdine Hill

The Tower

Dorstone Hill

Bredwardine Hill

RATING
4/10

FAIR VIEW

CROESAU BACH, SHROPSHIRE

Is there a better route into England than this? I'm not sure, but what a perfect introduction to the country's hills. Leaving Wales behind – not that there is any fanfare or sign of a border – you cross a small stream and begin to climb. The lower slopes are a solid grind, over 10% and rising in a straight line to the first of the two significant hairpin bends. The pitch relents a touch allowing you to turn to your left and take in the stunning views out over the country you've left behind. The gradient won't ever really get on top of you on this climb, but it will test you. Continuing upwards, kinking slightly left and right, you reach the second, fantastic right-hand hairpin. Get out of the saddle and power through it to begin the final stretch (which isn't as tough as the lower slopes). You finish as you pass an amazing house with the most enviable views imaginable.

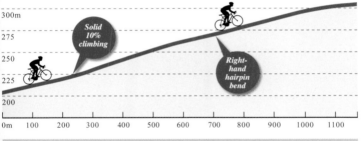

Solid 10% climbing

Right-hand hairpin bend

300m
275
250
225
200

0m 100 200 300 400 500 600 700 800 900 1000 1100

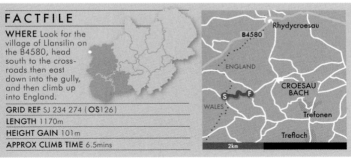

FACTFILE

WHERE Look for the village of Llansilin on the B4580, head south to the cross-roads then east down into the gully, and then climb up into England.

GRID REF SJ 234 274 (OS126)

LENGTH 1170m

HEIGHT GAIN 101m

APPROX CLIMB TIME 6.5mins

Rhydycroesau
B4580
ENGLAND
CROESAU BACH
WALES
Trefonen
Treflach
2km

PLAS PENTRE

CROESAU BACH, SHROPSHIRE

This little corner of England between Oswestry and the Welsh border is a maze of tiny twisting roads, and most of them are steep. From Blodwell Bank rising out of Porth-y-waen to the climb up Baker's Hill out of Rhydycroesau, you'll find a host of testing gradients, and lying in the middle is this nasty climb. Even though it's less than a kilometre long, the slope averages over 12%, which more than makes up for its diminutive length. Cross the River Morda and ahead you see a sign that says unsuitable for motor vehicles, but as you hit the initial punishing 15% ramp, it might just as well read unsuitable for tired legs. There is a slight cessation in the savagery as you pass between some farmhouses, and then it kicks up once more – the narrow, dirty and rough road seemingly gripping your tyres. Gradually the slope begins to recede, but there's one final push to the left before you make the junction at the top.

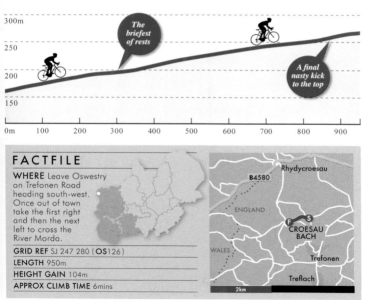

The briefest of rests

A final nasty kick to the top

FACTFILE

WHERE Leave Oswestry on Trefonen Road heading south-west. Once out of town take the first right and then the next left to cross the River Morda.

GRID REF SJ 247 280 (OS126)

LENGTH 950m

HEIGHT GAIN 104m

APPROX CLIMB TIME 6mins

Rhydycroesau
B4580
ENGLAND
CROESAU BACH
WALES
Trefonen
Treflach
2km

THE WREKIN

WELLINGTON, SHROPSHIRE

West of Telford lies the Wrekin – a lone giant protruding from the surrounding landscape. Such is its dominance on the horizon that it holds a special place in local folklore. Not the hardest climb in the land, it is nevertheless the most significant in this part of England and a serious challenge. There are two ways up and over, neither of which takes you to the top – that can be reached only by foot. To tackle the climb from the north, leave the Wrekin car park and climb gently through the woods at the base of a large rock face. The surface is rough and bumpy as you wind your way through a dense tunnel of trees and the climb steepens as you approach the exit of the forest. With the Wrekin on your right, the road flattens and the surface improves, rising hard again as you pass some farmhouses. Bending right then left, the last push will have your legs burning by the time you reach the top and roll down into Little Wenlock.

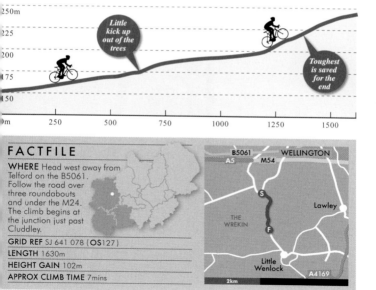

Little kick up out of the trees

Toughest is saved for the end

FACTFILE

WHERE Head west away from Telford on the B5061. Follow the road over three roundabouts and under the M24. The climb begins at the junction just past Cluddley.

GRID REF SJ 641 078 (OS127)

LENGTH 1630m

HEIGHT GAIN 102m

APPROX CLIMB TIME 7mins

JIGGERS BANK

IRONBRIDGE, SHROPSHIRE

Jiggers Bank rises from Ironbridge Gorge, considered by many to be the birthplace of the Industrial Revolution. Heading north from the bridge you begin the climbing into Coalbrookdale, gently at first, away from the valley and the River Severn. Although this is the major route out of the gorge, it's not a busy one; however, there is a set of traffic lights to negotiate at a narrowing in the road, so be prepared for a slight delay. Shortly after the lights you have the option to turn left to take a narrow, twisting route up the same ridge, but stick to the larger road for a better climbing experience. Passing under a railway bridge on to Jiggers Bank, the long, straight 10% slog out of the gorge leads to a beautifully smooth set of sweeping bends. Passing through these corners, the gradient never slackens. Continue round to the right to the finish – which is even steeper – at the junction with the roundabout.

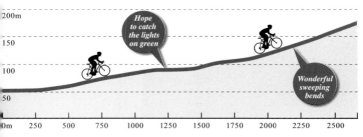

Hope to catch the lights on green

Wonderful sweeping bends

FACTFILE

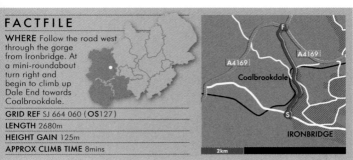

WHERE Follow the road west through the gorge from Ironbridge. At a mini-roundabout turn right and begin to climb up Dale End towards Coalbrookdale.

GRID REF	SJ 664 060 (OS127)
LENGTH	2680m
HEIGHT GAIN	125m
APPROX CLIMB TIME	8mins

CALLOW LANE

MINSTERLEY, SHROPSHIRE

Travelling south-east from Minsterley heading towards the mighty Long Mynd ('Long Mountain'), Callow Lane is an excellent way to enter the north Shropshire Hills. Leaving the A488 you're soon out of the small town and the slope rises in front of you just past a turn on the left. Stepping up steeply, easing, and then getting steeper again, it delivers you to a sharp right-hand corner that leads to a slight plateau. Compose yourself and look up ahead to the widening of the road before it rises rapidly once more. You next begin a long-drawn-out bend to the left before weaving between the wonderfully gnarled trees, crumbling walls, and rolling grassland. As you rise, make sure to glance over your right shoulder and take in the views – a just reward for your efforts thus far. To finish, the climb bends right, heading south-east to end just round the pronounced brow past the farm buildings on your right.

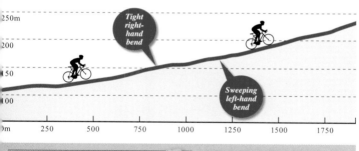

FACTFILE

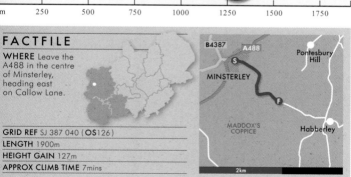

WHERE Leave the A488 in the centre of Minsterley, heading east on Callow Lane.

GRID REF SJ 387 040 (OS126)	
LENGTH 1900m	
HEIGHT GAIN 127m	
APPROX CLIMB TIME 7mins	

RATING 7/10

THE LONG MYND

LEEBOTWOOD, SHROPSHIRE

Having already bagged The Burway and Asterton Bank, I was keen to check out this ascent: the long way up The Long Mynd ('Long Mountain'). You begin in Leebotwood on the gentle lower slopes rising away from the A49. When you reach Woolstaston there's a slight blip in the profile, as bending through the village you'll briefly need to leave the saddle. Not long after leaving the village, though, any notion that this would be a sedate ascent is blown out of the water. In front of you stands a colossal 20% ramp. Focus on the crossroads sign at the top and drag yourself past it to continue on yet more punishing gradient. Looking out over the grand views to your right, you can return to the saddle to cross the cattle grid and enter The Long Mynd moorland. Suddenly it's wild and open, but you may be disappointed by the finale; the climb seems to fizzle to nothing. Thankfully, the lower slopes more than make up for it.

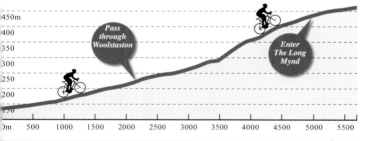

Pass through Woolstaston

Enter The Long Mynd

450m
400
350
300
250
200
150

0m   500   1000   1500   2000   2500   3000   3500   4000   4500   5000   5500

FACTFILE

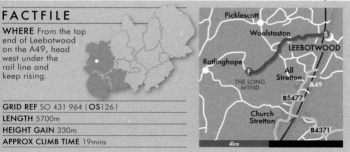

WHERE From the top end of Leebotwood on the A49, head west under the rail line and keep rising.

Picklescott
Woolstaston
LEEBOTWOOD
Ratlinghope
All Stretton
THE LONG MYND
A49
B5477
Church Stretton
B4371
4km

GRID REF SO 431 964 (OS126)

LENGTH 5700m

HEIGHT GAIN 330m

APPROX CLIMB TIME 19mins

THE BURWAY

CHURCH STRETTON, SHROPSHIRE

Leave Church Stretton and head west up the minor road on to The Long Mynd, ('Long Mountain') which dominates the skyline. As soon as you begin, bending to the right, you are warned of the 20% gradient ahead. The climb is steep to begin with but levels off slightly past numerous houses, before getting steeper again as it crosses a cattle grid to enter the wilderness. The coarse but well-maintained narrow road rises at 20% like a tarmac ledge perched on the side of the mountain; to the left there's a vertical bank, to the right a precipitous drop. As the road veers out of the steepest section a guard rail forms a barrier against the abyss. Here you enter an easier section that snakes with the same coarse surface as the earlier slope and which leads to a fake brow, from where you can build momentum. The climb isn't over yet, though – you still have to pass a couple of car parks to finish alongside the largest one, on your right.

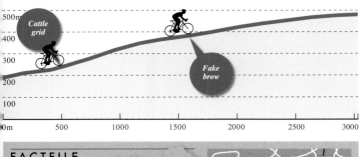

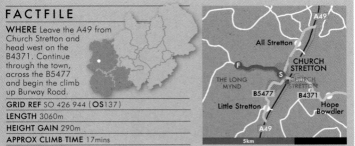

FACTFILE

WHERE Leave the A49 from Church Stretton and head west on the B4371. Continue through the town, across the B5477 and begin the climb up Burway Road.

GRID REF SO 426 944 (OS137)

LENGTH 3060m

HEIGHT GAIN 290m

APPROX CLIMB TIME 17mins

RATING
10/10

ASTERTON BANK

ASTERTON, SHROPSHIRE

On the western edge of the Long Mynd lies the infamous Asterton Bank; although it is also known by many other names, there are none that I can print here. Without being too hysterical, this climb is nothing more than a joyless straight line of pain. Start opposite the old red telephone box, roll past the numerous warning signs and across the cattle grid, and then bend slightly left. You're now face-to-face with the vicious 25% corner, which takes you on to the cruel slopes that cling to the side of the sheer bank. The surface, just wide enough for a single car, is smooth at the edges but little more than gravel and moss in the centre. It never relents, never lets up, until you reach a bend in the shadow of a rocky outcrop; you've still a fair bit of climbing to reach the top, but it's not as hard from here. You will be able to reacquaint your backside with the saddle for the final push to the summit on the approach to the gliding club.

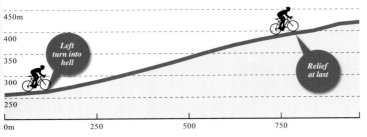

Left turn into hell

Relief at last

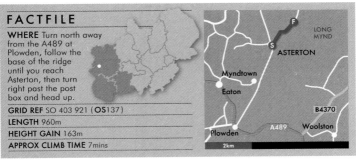

FACTFILE

WHERE Turn north away from the A489 at Plowden, follow the base of the ridge until you reach Asterton, then turn right past the post box and head up.

GRID REF SO 403 921 (OS137)

LENGTH 960m

HEIGHT GAIN 163m

APPROX CLIMB TIME 7mins

SPOAD HILL

NEWCASTLE, SHROPSHIRE

What a dirty old road, and what a savage, remorseless little climb. The first time I rode Spoad Hill I was blissfully unaware of what torture lay ahead. I rolled into Newcastle on the B4368 and as soon as I turned left I hit a wall. Click, click, click, down to the largest sprocket, you grind up to a muddy plateau through a farmyard. Gather yourself here because as soon as you leave it is immediately tough once more, although the condition of the surface does improve a degree. The centre of the road is covered with a substantial amount of debris as you force your way past the twisted tree roots that protrude from the muddy banks. Bending steadily right, it's a real morale breaker, as the gradient hardly ever wavers from its constant punishment. The summit comes at the end of a huge amount of toil; the higher slopes are not quite as steep as those lower down, but by then you will be beyond caring.

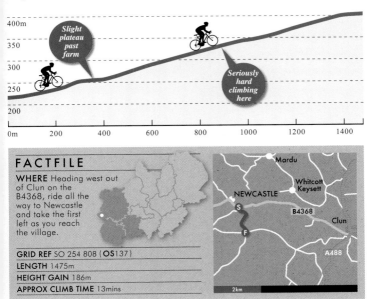

FACTFILE

WHERE Heading west out of Clun on the B4368, ride all the way to Newcastle and take the first left as you reach the village.

GRID REF SO 254 808 (**OS**137)
LENGTH 1475m
HEIGHT GAIN 186m
APPROX CLIMB TIME 13mins

ABDON BURF

DITTON PRIORS, SHROPSHIRE

The masts on top of Brown Clee Hill are visible for many miles in all directions; they dominate the skyline and the climb to reach them redefines suffering. The road is closed to traffic so you have to open the gate first, and then lined out ahead are 800m of the most horrendous climbing anywhere in Britain. This road broke my mind before it broke my body; it forced me to dismount and walk not once, but three times. So savage is its slope, so utterly unforgiving, I simply could not face the pain. There isn't a degree of variation in pitch, and not an inch of waver from its line until a cattle grid appears ahead. Try and muster the speed to cross it and you'll enter rolling grassland nestled high above the surrounding agricultural land. Pick your way through the twists and turns to finish at the base of the twin towers and soak up what is arguably the finest 360-degree view in the whole of England.

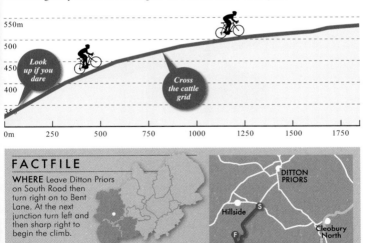

FACTFILE

WHERE Leave Ditton Priors on South Road then turn right on to Bent Lane. At the next junction turn left and then sharp right to begin the climb.

GRID REF SO 594 866 (OS137)

LENGTH 1850m

HEIGHT GAIN 208m

APPROX CLIMB TIME 12mins

CLUNTON COPPICE

CLUNTON, SHROPSHIRE

The climb up into Clunton Coppice is a degree easier than the torturous Spoad Hill a few kilometres to the east (see page 138), but nonetheless a fearsome and rewarding climb. Leave the village and cross the river; you rise slightly and ahead the road bends left and up the bank. Lying at the base of a gorge flanked by high, muddy, hedge-topped banks, the narrow, rough, and broken road cuts its course upwards. This opening stretch soon curves round to the right and promptly gets steeper and rougher. The initial punishing ramps will hurt the legs, but thankfully there's a slight dip and a mini-plateau as you enter the Coppice. Make the most of this relief, as it's disappointingly short-lived. The climbing continues shortly after on a debris-covered surface. In the shadow of the moss-covered rocks you soon reach a tight right-hand corner that touches 20% at its steepest before easing and bending left to finish.

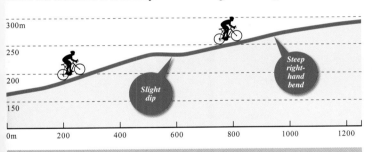

300m

250

200

Slight
dip

Steep
right-
hand
bend

150

0m   200   400   600   800   1000   1200

FACTFILE

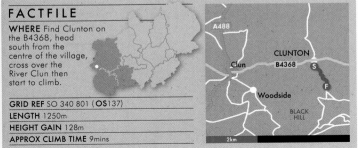

WHERE Find Clunton on the B4368, head south from the centre of the village, cross over the River Clun then start to climb.

A488

CLUNTON

Clun   B4368   S

Woodside   F

BLACK
HILL

2km

GRID REF SO 340 801 (**OS**137)

LENGTH 1250m

HEIGHT GAIN 128m

APPROX CLIMB TIME 9mins

RATING
4/10

WENLOCK EDGE

MUCH WENLOCK, SHROPSHIRE

There are a handful of ways to climb the ridge up into Much Wenlock. The main road – the A458 – is a great climb, but it's a bit busy, so I recommend this back route. Leaving the A458 at Harley you drop into the valley and find the climb's base at the ford. But this is no ordinary ford: it's a monster, so resist the temptation to ride through it and take the footpath instead. From here the road rises, snaking gently into Homer. There's a substantial dip through the village and then the climb starts to show its true character. First up, there's a harsh left-hand bend and then the road sweeps round another tough right-hand corner. As soon as you exit, you head left into the last of this series of challenging twists and turns. Ignore the 'slow' signs painted on the road and push on to the brow ahead, which lies just short of the junction with the A4169.

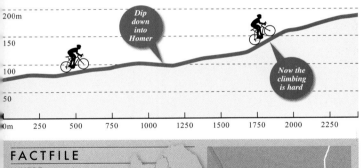

FACTFILE

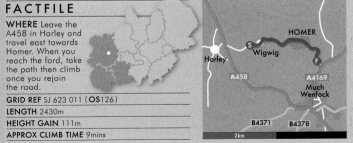

WHERE Leave the A458 in Harley and travel east towards Homer. When you reach the ford, take the path then climb once you rejoin the road.

GRID REF SJ 623 011 (**OS**126)

LENGTH 2430m

HEIGHT GAIN 111m

APPROX CLIMB TIME 9mins

CLEE HILL

CLEEHILL, SHROPSHIRE

The solitary Clee Hill sits just outside Ludlow – an isolated peak at the bottom end of the Shropshire Hills topped with a science-fiction-like radar station. Beginning at the T-junction opposite the Angel Bank Garage, the surface on the early slopes is a mess; there are holes within holes and patches upon patches, evidence of years of neglect and sub-standard repairs. It's fairly steep up to a group of houses where there's a little respite and then it's hard again to a cattle grid. The climb then eases and dips slightly to reach the base of the final push to the summit – not too steep, but still a challenge up to a plateau and a right-hand bend. Here you're greeted with a faded no entry sign. I kept riding through the decaying abandoned buildings, past the second no entry sign until I reached a third sign at the gates of the station compound where I finally got the message and turned back.

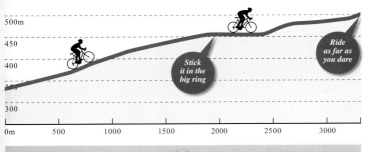

Stick it in the big ring

Ride as far as you dare

FACTFILE

WHERE Travelling east from Ludlow on the A4117, you reach the village of Cleehill. The climb starts at the left turn opposite the Angel Bank Garage on Dhustone Lane.

GRID REF SO 597 776 (**OS**137)

LENGTH 3350m

HEIGHT GAIN 185m

APPROX CLIMB TIME 14mins

ST KENELM'S PASS

CLENT, WORCESTERSHIRE

The globe is littered with great mountain passes; roads that traverse inhospitable terrain at challenging altitudes, forming vital links between communities, even countries – roads such as the Gotthard Pass, the Stelvio Pass, the Khyber Pass, and yes of course, St Kenelm's Pass, crossing the not quite so savage peaks of the Clent Hills. 'Pass' is quite an audacious moniker for such a seemingly insignificant road, but a pass it is and I've marked the start at the crossroads in Clent. From here it kicks up hitting 10%, and then backs off before climbing hard once more. For the majority of its course the slope is easy to deal with, although there are the odd spikes in the gradient to keep you on your toes. Winding through the woodland and rolling, grassy banks you line up for the summit, and to mirror the start there's another 10% ramp to tackle before you roll over to take in the views out over Birmingham.

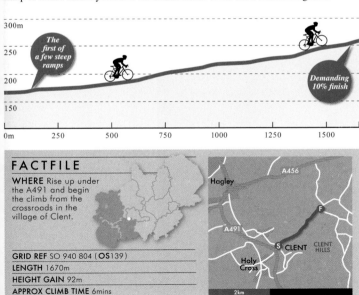

FACTFILE

WHERE Rise up under the A491 and begin the climb from the crossroads in the village of Clent.

GRID REF SO 940 804 (OS139)

LENGTH 1670m

HEIGHT GAIN 92m

APPROX CLIMB TIME 6mins

WINWOOD HEATH ROAD

GREAT FARLEY WOOD, WORCESTERSHIRE

Farley Lane is the obvious way up this ridge, but if you make the effort to find it among the tangle of dirty lanes, then this climb is far more rewarding. Following Shut Mill Lane and the brook that runs parallel with it, you reach Winwood Heath Road and it kicks up straight away. Within the first 100m you hit a 20% left-hand bend; force yourself around it and then sit back in the saddle to compose yourself for what lies ahead. Becoming gradually steeper, the narrow, quiet, and debris-covered road begins to bend right. Although it's never as tough as that first bend, it is still a demanding climb that offers little opportunity to rest. Yes, the gradient eases in a number of places, but it steps back up once again until you break free from the woodland to approach the summit. Once you reach the top – the junction with Farley Road – make sure you turn around for the stunning views out over the Malvern Hills.

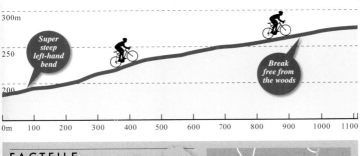

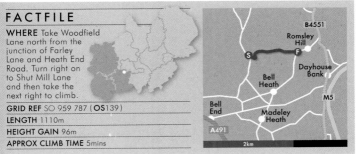

FACTFILE

WHERE Take Woodfield Lane north from the junction of Farley Lane and Heath End Road. Turn right on to Shut Mill Lane and then take the next right to climb.

GRID REF SO 959 787 (**OS**139)

LENGTH 1110m

HEIGHT GAIN 96m

APPROX CLIMB TIME 5mins

RATING
5/10

BEACON HILL

LICKEY, WORCESTERSHIRE

I came to this southern suburb of Birmingham to have a look at Rose Hill on the B4096, but a bit of local knowledge directed my attention slightly to the west. Rose Hill is a substantial test, but it's busy, and my guide was correct – this is a quieter and, yes, steeper road. Leave Leach Heath Lane and rise gently through the houses until you see the zigzag road sign ahead, where the slope ramps violently up in front of you. Hit this stretch at speed and if you're very lucky you'll still be well on top of your gear when the course breaks hard right, leading to a welcome easing. As you approach the second pronounced bend, the road is lined with a barrier on the right-hand side and you sweep back on yourself as the gradient begins to bite once more. You'll be breathing hard now and will have to put in a proper effort to reach the brow ahead, which, although not the summit, is just 500m shy of it nestled in the Lickey Hills.

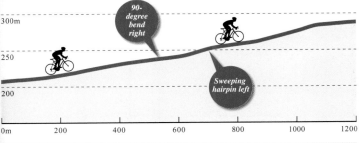

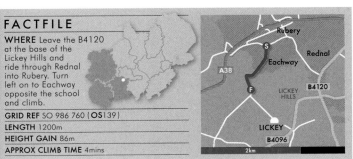

FACTFILE

WHERE Leave the B4120 at the base of the Lickey Hills and ride through Rednal into Rubery. Turn left on to Eachway opposite the school and climb.

GRID REF SO 986 760 (OS139)

LENGTH 1200m

HEIGHT GAIN 86m

APPROX CLIMB TIME 4mins

RATING
8/10

WYNNIATTS WAY

Boy does this hill have a nasty surprise up its sleeve. Locals will be well aware of its delights and will come mentally prepared, but riding it for the first time is a proper shock to the system. Once you've found the base in Abberley the road rises gradually steeper away from a couple of houses. Yes it's hard here but not too challenging, and you'll be asking yourself what all the fuss is about. Ahead you see a brow where the road appears to head straight over it, but you'll notice it's a dead end and in fact you must head right. Here is where it hits you, out of nowhere, just around the 90-degree corner – you're faced with a wall. Easily 20%, it will have you furiously clicking down through the gears and hoping you have the strength to make it to the bend ahead. While your legs are screaming, the road kinks right and continues on a punishing pitch, up through the woods all the way to the abrupt summit.

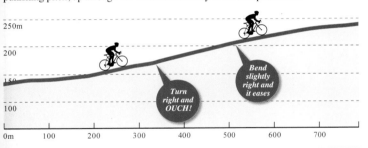

FACTFILE

WHERE Head east from the B4202 through the village of Abberley. Turn right just before the Manor Arms Inn and take the third right after this to reach the base.

GRID REF SO 749 673 (OS150)

LENGTH 790m

HEIGHT GAIN 105m

APPROX CLIMB TIME 5mins

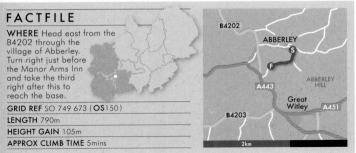

ANKERDINE HILL

KNIGHTWICK, WORCESTERSHIRE

The moment you arrive at the base of Ankerdine Hill you're met with the dramatic warning that tells HGV drivers to engage their crawler gear. This is a sure sign you are in for a treat, so long as you're not trapped behind a truck that is. From the abrupt corner outside The Talbot Hotel it's not long before you're rampaging through the gears to help you cope with the solid 17% gradient. Thankfully there's a brief lull after 100m, a minute break in hostilities before it ramps up once more. This time the strength-sapping gradient lasts much longer, and by now it won't be just the HGVs that will be using their crawler gear – most likely you will be too. The second light easing comes as you pass a junction down to the left and from here you can see the top. Focus ahead on the buildings, in particular the cottage with its medieval tower, as once you've rounded the corner in front of it, it's all over.

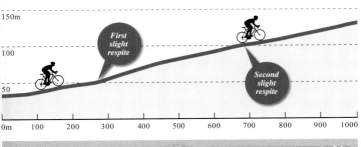

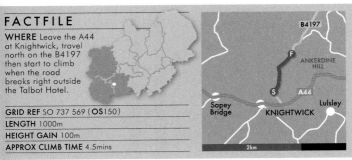

FACTFILE

WHERE Leave the A44 at Knightwick, travel north on the B4197 then start to climb when the road breaks right outside the Talbot Hotel.

GRID REF SO 737 569 (**OS**150)

LENGTH 1000m

HEIGHT GAIN 100m

APPROX CLIMB TIME 4.5mins

WALWYN ROAD

COLWALL STONE, HEREFORDSHIRE

The Malvern Hills, famous for their mineral water, are visible for miles and miles, forming a large rocky outcrop that protrudes from the surrounding plains. At first glance one would expect to find a climber's paradise, but I was a little disappointed. There are many routes to ride up from the east and the west, but none right to the top – that privilege is reserved for walkers. The best I found, although likely a bit busier than Harcourth Road to the north, is Walwyn Road. You begin on the western side in Colwall Stone where the slope picks up as you head north-east, getting steeper as you progress. Riding into Upper Colwall, you reach a zigzag and the toughest section of the climb. Bending tight right and then shortly after tighter left, the corners are fantastic. Now you line up for the summit, which cuts into the rock – as pronounced a brow as you'll find, and also the border with Worcestershire.

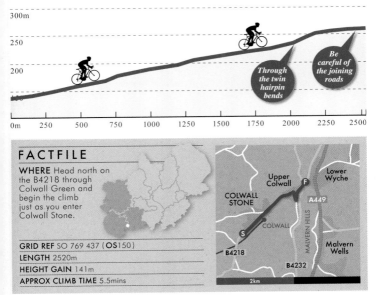

Through the twin hairpin bends

Be careful of the joining roads

FACTFILE

WHERE Head north on the B4218 through Colwall Green and begin the climb just as you enter Colwall Stone.

GRID REF SO 769 437 (**OS**150)

LENGTH 2520m

HEIGHT GAIN 141m

APPROX CLIMB TIME 5.5mins

BREDWARDINE HILL

BREDWARDINE, HEREFORDSHIRE

This long climb has a killer start, so get ready to grind. Leave the B4352 in Bredwardine, just after the Red Lion Hotel and the 25% gradient sign; straight away, you're climbing. Up ahead, the road gets steeper and steeper and steeper, until you're stranded on the promised arc of 25% tarmac searching for an extra sprocket to preserve your forward motion. Passing the saltbox on your right, and snaking left and right across the road, you line up for the final savage stretch to the brow ahead, where the severity of the slope finally recedes. From here on, the climbing isn't so tough, but the damage to the legs has already been done. Next you enter a distinctive horseshoe-shaped bend that curves round a collection of hillside houses and you've almost reached the end of the climbing. Bending left, the remainder to the summit is very gentle and fizzles out just as you reach the final 90-degree left-hand bend.

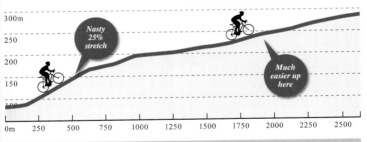

Nasty 25% stretch

Much easier up here

FACTFILE

WHERE Ride into Bredwardine on the B4352 and then head west up Bredwardine Hill, just after Red Lion Hotel.

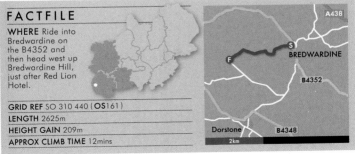

GRID REF SO 310 440 (OS161)

LENGTH 2625m

HEIGHT GAIN 209m

APPROX CLIMB TIME 12mins

DORSTONE HILL

One look at the Strava leaderboard and you can instantly tell this climb's been used in a big race, as proper riders have laid down some proper times and placed the KOM (King of the Mountain title) well out of the reach of us mortals. Although a kilometre shorter than its neighbour Bredwardine Hill (see page 161), it still gains close to the same gradient, so you know it will hurt. Never easy, the slope steps up the ridge, the pitch alternating between a manageable 7–8% and a more substantial 15%, and in places hitting close to 20%. The further you climb up through the woods, the tougher the steep bits become. As you pass a turn on your right the sky opens. From here you've one last sweeping stretch right before a plateau, where you'll assume it's all over until you glance up to see yet another little ramp. This is the last thing you need as the legs will be jelly, but dig deep and give it one last effort to crest the summit.

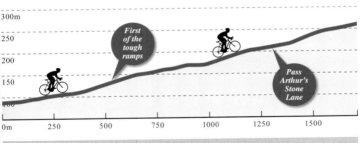

First of the tough ramps

Pass Arthur's Stone Lane

300m
250
200
150
100

0m   250   500   750   1000   1250   1500

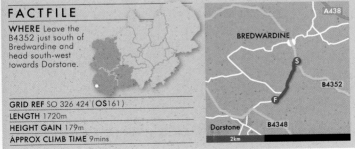

FACTFILE

WHERE Leave the B4352 just south of Bredwardine and head south-west towards Dorstone.

A438
BREDWARDINE
S
B4352
B4348
Dorstone

2km

GRID REF SO 326 424 (**OS**161)

LENGTH 1720m

HEIGHT GAIN 179m

APPROX CLIMB TIME 9mins

THE TOWER

If you take a look on Landranger 161 just south of Dorstone, you'll see the unmistakable symbol for a radio mast, and then you'll also see there's a paved road leading up to it. This is like a red rag to a bull in my world; these are always challenging roads, so I had to check it out. The base lies just outside of Dorstone where the climb starts gently, rolling slightly. As you approach a dead end sign it banks right and the hard work begins. The stiff gradient comes in waves as you pass a number of lone houses, peaking at 25% past the last one. Once over these punishing ramps the road bends left and lines up dead straight to the summit. You can see the tower on top of the hill and you only have a short stretch of easy climbing before the final grind to the top. It's not clear at first, but there's a gate halfway up for you to open (just a slight inconvenience) before you reach the tower and stand on the top of Vagar Hill.

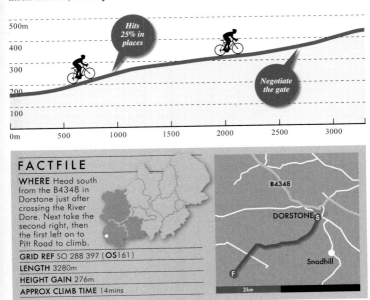

FACTFILE

WHERE Head south from the B4348 in Dorstone just after crossing the River Dore. Next take the second right, then the first left on to Pitt Road to climb.

GRID REF SO 288 397 (OS161)

LENGTH 3280m

HEIGHT GAIN 276m

APPROX CLIMB TIME 14mins

VOWCHURCH COMMON

VOWCHURCH, HEREFORDSHIRE

I'm comfortably rolling along the B4348 heading back to the car after a long ride, the wind on my back and a few climbs in my legs, when out of the corner of my eye I spot a red triangle. I slam the anchors on, and turn round to have a closer look: wow – 25% – time to leave this dull, flat road and head upwards. And what a find this road was. The legs that had previously been turning that big gear on the flat are soon screaming as they ride away from the crossroads, up to the right-hand kink where the slope hits 25%. This short yet vicious ramp between houses and past driveways leads you left. Steep round the corner, it thankfully eases through the village, allowing you to sit down and take stock before you hit the next 25% slopes. Ouch again – twisting a little left and right, pull yourself to the brow, force the bike over, and then power on across the plateau to the summit, just shy of the right-hand junction.

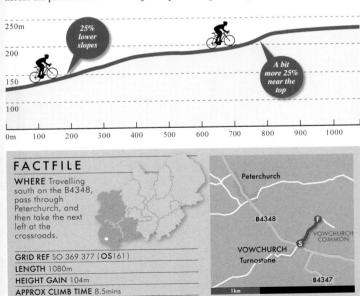

FACTFILE

WHERE Travelling south on the B4348, pass through Peterchurch, and then take the next left at the crossroads.

GRID REF SO 369 377 (OS161)
LENGTH 1080m
HEIGHT GAIN 104m
APPROX CLIMB TIME 8.5mins

BLACK DARREN

LONGTOWN, HEREFORDSHIRE

Leaving the top end of Longtown, you turn left to plummet down to cross the brook at the base of the Olchon Valley. Spanning the horizon ahead of you stands Black Darren, an impenetrable wall of rock forming a physical border between England and Wales. Following the rapid descent, you swing round a corner and immediately ramp back up; passing a farmhouse on your right, the slope hits close to 20% on the bend before easing. It's not long before it is steep again up to the next buildings, round another right-hand bend, and the struggle continues. Creeping ever closer to the towering barrier ahead, you reach a final collection of buildings and a sustained stretch of tough gradient. By now you can see that the road doesn't, thankfully, make it all the way to the top of the ridge, but bends abruptly right to climb for a few metres more before plateauing.

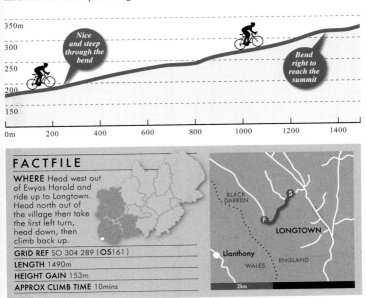

Nice and steep through the bend

Bend right to reach the summit

350m
300
250
200
150

0m   200   400   600   800   1000   1200   1400

FACTFILE

WHERE Head west out of Ewyas Harold and ride up to Longtown. Head north out of the village then take the first left turn, head down, then climb back up.

GRID REF SO 304 289 (OS161)

LENGTH 1490m

HEIGHT GAIN 153m

APPROX CLIMB TIME 10mins

BLACK DARREN

S

F

LONGTOWN

Llanthony

WALES   ENGLAND

2km

RIDE THEM ALL

IT WOULD BE RUDE NOT TO

You're never too far from a great hill anywhere in the Midlands, even if you happen to be stranded on the plains of Lincolnshire. The key is knowing where they are, and now that you have a copy of this book in your hands, their locations are a mystery no more. Of course, the climbs of the Lincolnshire Wolds aren't quite as challenging as the precipitous slopes of the Peak District or the savage inclines of the Long Mynd, but they are still well worth exploring. If you've already been ticking off the climbs in the original *100 Greatest Cycling Climbs* and its sequel, *Another 100 Greatest Cycling Climbs*, then you can transfer those ticks to this list. Or why not ride them again and beat your previous time, or even attempt a King of the Mountain title? They will be more than happy to welcome you back. So get out your maps, pick a base, plan a route, and head for the hills.

EAST MIDLANDS

Hill	Date Ridden	Time
Normanby Rise		
Red Hill		
Tetford Hill		
Michaelgate		
Leadenham Hill		
Cocking Hill		
Eakring Hill		
Oxton Bank		
Georges Hill		
Terrace Hill		
Lings Hill		
Beacon Hill		
Polly Bott's Lane		
Launde Abbey		
Kings Hill		
Rockingham Hill		

CHECKLIST

DERBYSHIRE

Hill	Date Ridden	Time
Carr Lane		
Hardwick Hill		
Slack Hill		
Jaggers Lane		
Bank Road		
Riber		
Holly Lane		
Rowsley Bar		
Beeley Moor		
Curbar Edge		
Burbage Moor		
Manners Wood		
Monsal Head		
Winnats Pass		
Mam Nick		
Snake Pass		
Monks' Road		
Eccles Pike		
Peaslows		
Axe Edge		

WEST MIDLANDS PART ONE

Hill	Date Ridden	Time
Gun Hill		
Thorncliffe Bank		
Larkstone Lane		
Ilam Moor		
Biddulph Moor		
Lask Edge		
Mow Cop		
Foxt Lane		

Hill	Date Ridden	Time
Carr Bank		
Marchington Cliff		
Hanbury Hill		
Stile Cop		
Larkstoke Hill		
Whichford Hill		
Edge Hill		

WEST MIDLANDS PART TWO

Hill	Date Ridden	Time
Fair View		
Plas Pentre		
The Wrekin		
Jiggers Bank		
Callow Lane		
The Long Mynd		
The Burway		
Asterton Bank		
Spoad Hill		
Abdon Burf		
Clunton Coppice		
Wenlock Edge		
Clee Hill		
St Kenelm's Pass		
Winwood Heath Road		
Beacon Hill		
Wynniatts Way		
Ankerdine Hill		
Walwyn Road		
Bredwardine Hill		
Dorstone Hill		
The Tower		
Vowchurch Common		
Black Darren		

Ride them all.

BRITISH
CLIMBING
GUIDES
ALREADY
AVAILABLE

SNAKE PASS
Long descent
1 in 14

Low gear
for 1 mile

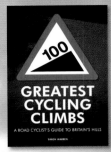

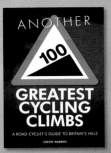

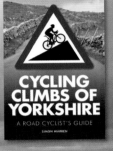